Stud
Fully re
C000125199

Your Life

The whole-school solution for PSHE and Citizenship

John Foster, Simon Foster and Kim Richardson

William Collins' dream of knowledge for all began with the publication of his first book in 1819. A self-educated mill worker, he not only enriched millions of lives, but also founded a flourishing publishing house. Today, staying true to his spirit, Collins books are packed with inspiration, innovation and practical expertise. They place you at the centre of a world of possibility and give you exactly what you need to explore it.

Collins. Do more.

Published by Collins
An imprint of HarperCollinsPublishers
1 London Bridge Street
London
SE1 9GF

Browse the complete Collins catalogue at
www.collins.co.uk

British Library Cataloguing in Publication Data
A Catalogue record for this book is available from the British Library.

Commissioned by Emily Pither

Project managed by Mike Appleton

Edited by Kim Richardson

Design by Jordan Publishing Design

Layout by Jouve

Cover design by Angela English

Cover photo by Dougal Waters/Getty Images

Printed in Italy by Grafica Veneta S.p.A

Production by Robin Forrester

Acknowledgements

The Publishers gratefully acknowledge the following for permission to reproduce copyright material. While every effort has been made to trace the copyright holders, in cases where this has been unsuccessful or if any have inadvertently been overlooked, the Publishers will be pleased to make the necessary arrangements at the first opportunity.

Text extracts: p6: Teenagers react against anything goes society' by Rebecca Allison, The Guardian, 11 March, 2004 © Guardian Newspapers Limited 2004. Used with permission; p7: 'Katie believes in God and marriage. Her mother doesn't' by Liz Lightfoot, The Telegraph, 11 March, 2004 © Telegraph Newspapers 2004. Reprinted with permission; p9: Adapted from 'Breakthough in human cloning offers new transport hope' by Sarah Knapton, The Telegraph, 17 April 2014; p11: 'Passive revision and Active revision' from The Student's Guide to Exam Success by Eileen Tracy, Reproduced with the kind permission of Open University Press. All rights reserved; p12: 'Beat exam stress' taken from the TEENS section of the BBC website www.bbc.co.uk/teens. Reprinted with the kind permission of the TEENS/BBC site; p12: Extract from Study Skills: a Pupil's Survival Guide by Christine Ostler, published by Ammonite Books. Reprinted with permission; p13: Extract from Study Skills: a Pupil's Survival Guide by Christine Ostler, published by Ammonite Books. Reprinted with permission; p14: 'Attitudes to marriage and cohabitation' from www.civitas.org.uk Reprinted with permission; p14: 'The myth of common law marriage', adapted from http://www.oneplusone.org.uk/content_topic/married-or-not/married-civil-partnered-or-not-the-legal-differences/; p16: Extract 'Be A Perfect Partner' from www.bbc.co.uk/radio1/onelife. Reprinted with permission of BBC/Onelife; p17: 'The Wedding Planners – Think you know the facts about about arranged marriages? Sunna Nasrullah sets you straight'. From www.exposure.org.uk Reprinted with permission; p18: 'Charlie's Story', from Meet the parents: Stories of teenage pregnancy and parenthood in Lewisham, The Young Foundation; p20: 'Being a parent' information supplied by Parentline Plus. Reprinted with permission; p21: 'What is a Mother?' from Smells of Childhood by Mary Donoghue, published by Brewin Books Ltd. Reprinted with permission; p21: Quote by Richard, aged 19, from Baby Fathers: New Images of Teenage Fatherhood by Edmund Clark. Reprinted with permission; p23: 'Case study: Kay', Adapted from the Newcastle College website, www.ncl-coll.ac.uk; p24: 'What are apprenticeships?' from www.apprenticeships.org.uk; p24: 'Case study: Ikrah', adapted from the Rotherham College website, www.rotherham.ac.uk; p25: 'Case study: Wilson', adapted from the Barnet Southgate College website, www.barnetsouthgate.ac.uk; p26: 'Job applications' from 16 and Beyond © Hereford and Worcester Careers Service 2001; p45: Adapted from 'U.S. airman and his son were "harassed and threatened on social media by pro-ISIS trolls" after they posted pictures of a bombing raid on Iraq' by Kieran Corcoran, Mail Online, 8 October 2014; p45: 'Social networking is meant to be social', from wearesocialpeople.com; p49: Extract 'Why is homophobia damaging?' from Homosexuality by Rosalyn Chissick in The Just Seventeen Advice Book edited by Jenny Tucker published by W H Allen in 1987. Reprinted with the kind permission of the author; p52: Extract 'What is depression?' from The Young Person's Guide to Stress, produced by Depression Alliance. Reprinted with permission; p52: Extract 'Types of depression' from Everything you need to know about depression, produced by Depression Alliance. Reprinted with permission; p53: Extract from 'Do you ever feel depressed?' from A Young Mind's Booklet, produced by YoungMinds © YoungMinds 2003. Used with permission; p55: Extract from The lowdown on… STIs, J17, February 2004 pp58/59. Reprinted with permission of EMAP; p56: Extract from Sex Ed by Dr Miriam Stoppard, published by Dorling Kindersley 1997. Copyright © 1997 by Dorling Kindersley, text copyright © 1997 by Miriam Stoppard. Reprinted with permission; p57: Extract from Sexually Transmitted Diseases by Jo Whelan, Hodder Wayland 2001. Reprinted with permission of Hodder & Stoughton Ltd; p58: Extracts from Tell It Like It Is by Katie Masters published by Virgin Books Limited. Copyright © Katie Masters 2002. Reprinted with permission of Virgin Books Ltd; p61: Adapted from 'The terrible truth about cannabis' by Ben Spencer, Daily Mail, 7 October 2014; p63: 'The recovery position' text and artwork from www.redcross.org.uk reprinted with the kind permission of the British Red Cross; p68: 'Why Britain should stay in the EU', by Hugh Dixon, The Independent, 25 March 2014; p84: Extracts taken from The First Aid Manual 8th Edition, the Authorised manual of St John Ambulance, St Andrew's Ambulance Association and The British Red Cross Society, published by Dorling Kindersley Ltd. Reprinted with permission of the three societies and Dorling Kindersley Ltd; p91: 'CSV Make a Difference Day' case study reproduced with the kind permission of Community Service Volunteers; p96: Extract from 'Starting Work, Leaflet 1' in the moneymoneymoney series produced by the Citizenship Foundation; p103: 'Comfort Kumeah' case study from www.divinechocolate.com reproduced with the kind permission of Divine Chocolate

Images: p6: Raw Pixel/Shutterstock; p7: Rob Marmion/Shutterstock; p8: Ocskay Mark/Shutterstock; p9: anyaivanova/Shutterstock; p12: vlad.georgescu/Shutterstock; p13: bibiphoto/Shutterstock; p14: Steve Cukrov/Shutterstock; p15: Vstock/Alamy; p16: KieferPix/Shutterstock; p17: EPA European Pressphoto Agency b.v/Alamy; p18: Jenoche/Shutterstock; p19: Tany Litte/Shutterstock; p20, top: Sergii Votit/Shutterstock; p20, bottom: Malija/Shutterstock; p23, left: Mrovka/Shutterstock; p23, right: East/Shutterstock; p24: Rawpixel/Shutterstock; p25: Goodluz/Shutterstock; p26: Nonwarit/Shutterstock; p28: Ramzi Haidar/Getty; p29: Allstar Picture Library/Alamy; p30: Stephen Dorey ABIPP/Alamy; p31: Alexander Mazurkevich/Shutterstock; p32, top: Dona_Bozi/Shutterstock; p32, bottom: David Levenson; p34, left: Kaetana/Shutterstock; p34, right: Janine Weidel/Rex Features; p35: Ulrich Doering/Alamy; p36: Diptendu Dutta/Getty; p37: Joerg Boethling/Alamy; p38: Juliya Shangarey/Shutterstock; p39, top: Paul Pickard/Alamy; p39, bottom: Diversity Studio/Shutterstock; p41: Jeff Morgan 11/Alamy; p42: Nils Jorgensen/Rex Features; p43: Vitchanan Photography/Shutterstock; p44: Amanda Dowler/Rex; p45, top: Twin Design/Shutterstock; p45, bottom: Bloomua/Shutterstock; p46: Ron Chapple Studiios/Thinkstock; p47: Radius Images/Alamy; p48: Ship Factory/Shutterstock; p49: Joel Goodman/LNP/Rex Features; p51: Satyrenko/Shutterstock; p52: Adam Gregor/Shutterstock; p53: Kamira/Shutterstock; p54: Zoltan Kiraly/Shutterstock; p55: Axente Vlad/Shutterstock; p57: LoloStock/Shutterstock; p58: Photographee.eu/Shutterstock; p59: Pandemin/Shutterstock; p61: Jack Hobhouse/Alamy; p62: iStock/Thinkstock; p64: Michael Kemp/Alamy; p65: Science Photo Library/Alamy; p66: Itan1409/Shutterstock; p67: Alain Jocard/Getty; p68: Julie Pop/Shutterstock; p69, left: 360b/Shutterstock; p69, right: 67 Photo/Alamy; p70: e X p o s e/Shutterstock; p71, top: Alan J Jones/Alamy; p71, middle: Mykhaylo Palinchak/Shutterstock; p71, bottom: Horizons WWP/Alamy; p72: John Stillwell/PA; p74: Xinhua/Alamy; p75: Sia Kambou/Getty; p76: Janek Skarzynski/Getty; p77: Khamidulin Sergey/Shutterstock; p78: Medyan Dairieh/Corbis; p79, left: Laperruque/Alamy; p79, right: AFP/Getty; p80: Piero Cruciatti/Alamy; p81, top: Stefano Tinti/Shutterstock; p81, bottom: EPA/Shutterstock; p82: Apiguide/Shutterstock; p83: Pedrosala/Shutterstock; p84, top: R Gino Santa Maria/Shutterstock; p84, bottom: esbobeldjik/Shutterstock; p85, top: Artens/Shutterstock; p85, bottom: Gustavo Toledo/Shutterstock; p86: Robin Utrecht/NurPhoto/Corbis; p88: Yanis Idir/Alamy; p89: dpa picture alliance archive/Alamy; p90: Lisa F Young/Shutterstock; p91: CSV; p93: Hugo Felix/Shutterstock; p94: Sukharevskyy Dmytro/Shutterstock; p95: Zuma Press Inc/Alamy; p98: chinahbzyg/Shutterstock; p99: cristapper/Shutterstock; p100, left: bluebay/Shutterstock; p100: right: Graham Oliver/Alamy; p102, left: brux/Shutterstock; p102, right: Timothy A Clary/Getty; p103, top: JLRphotography/Shutterstock; p103, bottom: PathDoc/Shutterstock; p104: Vorobyeva/Shutterstock; p105, left: Zhao jian kang/Shutterstock; p105, right: SNEHIT/Shutterstock; p106, left: Chatchai Somwat/Shutterstock; p106, middle-left: 360b/Shutterstock; p106, middle-right 360b/Shutterstock; p106, right: dean bertoncelj/Shutterstock; p107: Paul Prescott/Shutterstock; p108, left: PSL Images/Alamy; p108, right: HOANG DINH NAM/Getty; p109: T Photography/Shutterstock

Contents

Your Life 5 is the second of two books which together form a comprehensive two-year course in Personal, Social and Health Education (PSHE) and Citizenship at Key Stage 4. The table shows how the fourteen PSHE units provide a PSHE programme that covers personal wellbeing, social education and health education for year 11, and the eight Citizenship units, meet the requirements of the National Curriculum for Citizenship at Key Stage 4, covering such topics as the UK's role in the world, the UK economy and money management.

Personal, Social and Health Education

Personal wellbeing – Understanding yourself and handling relationships	Social education – Responsibilities and values	Keeping healthy
These units concentrate on developing your self-knowledge and your ability to manage your emotions and how to handle relationships.	These units concentrate on exploring social issues and on developing an understanding of your responsibilities towards other people in society, your values and your opinions.	These units are designed to help you take care of your physical and mental health.
• Developing your own values • Managing your time and studies • Marriage and commitment • Parenthood and parenting • Thinking ahead – planning your future • Reviewing and recording your learning	• Human rights • Global challenges – poverty, health and education • Media matters • Challenging offensive behaviour	• Managing stress and dealing with depression • Safer sex • Drugs and drug taking • Emergency first aid

Citizenship

Citizenship – Becoming an active citizen

These units focus on the society in which you live, on its laws and government and on developing the skills you require to become an active citizen.

- The UK's role in the world
- Global challenges – wars, weapons and terrorism
- Global challenges – environmental issues
- Working for change
- Co-operating on a community project

Citizenship – Economic and financial capability

These units aim to help you to manage your money effectively, to learn about the world of work and to understand how the economy works.

- Managing your money
- The UK economy
- The global economy

Confronting social and moral issues

Aim To consider different opinions on social and moral issues, and to explore your own views and opinions

Attitudes and values

An important part of anyone's identity is the values they hold. Having values and opinions that are well thought out and deeply felt can give you strength both in yourself and in the world. So where do you stand on the big issues of today?

Teenagers react against 'anything goes' society

Binge-drinking, under-age sex and misbehaviour are commonly associated with teenagers, but young people are a lot more conservative than their elders might think, according to a survey by *Bliss* magazine. Five thousand teenagers, aged between 12 and 18, were interviewed. Here are some of the results:

Teenage attitudes

- Two-thirds thought there were too many abortions.
- Seven out of ten said cannabis should not be legalised.
- One in eight 15-year-olds said that having to pay tuition fees would put them off going to university.
- Eight out of ten thought 'bogus' asylum seekers should be sent back.
- 84% supported harsher sentences for adult criminals.
- 78% said ID cards should be introduced.
- 92% believed in marriage.
- 60% felt it was best for couples to marry before having children.

Patriotism

- 86% said they were proud to be British.
- 70% feared Britain's identity would be lost through further European integration.
- 87% said 'No' to the euro.

The monarchy

Two-thirds of the teenagers interviewed wanted to keep the royal family and Parliament rather than have a presidential republic, though Prince William was a more popular choice than his father to be king.

Helen Johnston, the editor of *Bliss*, said: "Teenagers like boundaries, they make them feel safe – but over the years they've been torn down… This survey is a damning indictment of the damage caused by the lax attitudes of adults inflicted on children."

Source: *The Guardian*

In pairs

1 Are you surprised by any of the results in the survey of teenagers' attitudes?

2 What do you think the editor of *Bliss* means when she says, "Teenagers like boundaries, they make them feel safe – but over the years they've been torn down"? Do you agree?

Proud to be British? ▶

KATIE BELIEVES IN GOD AND MARRIAGE – HER MOTHER DOESN'T

Katie Lodwidge's life revolves around hair, make-up, shoes and clothes, according to her mother. The 15-year-old reads teenage magazines, talks for hours to her friends, enjoys dancing, singing and aerobics, and hates tidying her bedroom.

But behind this façade of normal teenage behaviour, Katie has developed a keen sense of morality and conservative social attitudes that contrast with the more liberal views of her mother, Alyson Pratt, 38.

Katie believes strongly in marriage and hopes to walk down the aisle one day. She feels that it is all right for people to have children outside marriage if they love each other and are in a stable relationship, but she wants to get married first.

This surprises Alyson, a legal secretary, who says she did not marry Katie's father. "I don't believe in marriage in this day and age because things have changed and so many marriages end in the heartache and nastiness of divorce."

Katie believes in God. Her mother is an atheist. Katie is proud to be British, her mother is stumped by the question. Katie wants Britain to become more integrated with the rest of Europe whereas her mother is firmly against it.

Katie says abortion is a serious step only to be undertaken when there is a good reason. Alyson supports abortion on demand because it is a woman's right to choose.

On drugs, the teenager is against legalisation of cannabis because it will encourage young people to experiment and fail to stop the dealers who will buy up supplies to sell cut-price on the streets. She wants tougher penalties for drugs. Her mother says cannabis should be legalised. "People are going to get hold of it, whether it is against the law or not."

On tougher penalties for crime their views coincide and both would like to see the death penalty brought back for child killers.

Their views diverge again on whether there should be tougher penalties to discourage under-age sex. Katie thinks there should be, to act as a deterrent. Her mother says tougher sanctions would make no difference. "If they want to have sex they will do it and I blame parents. It's up to parents to educate their children about the dangers of under-age sex, not schools. I know of people who allow their 13- and 14-year-old daughters to entertain boyfriends in their bedrooms. That will never happen in this house!"

Source: *Daily Telegraph*

In groups

1 Make a list of the key points in the article above.

2 Do you agree that teenagers are often more conservative than their parents?

3 Choose three of the issues explored in the article and discuss your own views on them.

On your own

Create your own survey using six to ten of the issues covered in both articles. Think carefully about how you will phrase the questions and then ask the following people to answer your questionnaire:

- Two people your own age
- Two people who are middle-aged
- Two people who are over 60.

Do you notice that different age groups have different views? Present your findings in a class discussion.

Exploring social and moral issues

Aim To examine two social and moral dilemmas, and explore your own views and opinions

Assisted dying

House of Lords split over assisted dying legislation

The assisted dying bill, proposed by the former Lord Chancellor Charles Falconer, would allow doctors to prescribe a lethal dose to patients with less than six months to live. By the end of the emotional 10-hour debate, a narrow majority of peers had spoken in favour of the legislation.

Supporters of the bill, who included former Archbishop of Canterbury George Carey, argued that it would end the terrible suffering of the terminally ill. They also raised the rights of individuals to choose their own fate.

Opponents of the bill, including paralympian Tanni Grey-Thompson, warned it would lead to pressure on disabled people not to be a burden on relatives. A few compared assisted dying with the mass euthanasia perpetrated by the Nazis.

The present law

Assisted dying, or assisted suicide, is the term used when doctors or relatives give patients drugs to kill themselves. At the moment it is outlawed in the UK. Helping someone to die could put you in prison for 14 years.

However, the law has not been applied for many years, even though nearly 250 Britons have travelled to Swiss clinics to end their lives.

The law elsewhere

Assisted dying is legal in Switzerland. Hundreds of patients have ended their lives in Dignitas clinics there. They are seen by doctors and lawyers before they are allowed to commit suicide. Euthanasia itself is illegal in Switzerland.

Assisted dying and voluntary euthanasia have been legal in the Netherlands since 2002. There are tight regulations, but concern has been raised about the escalation in the number of assisted deaths, which have increased by 15% a year since 2008.

In pairs

Discuss what you have learnt about assisted dying in this article. Why do you think Lord Falconer wants to change the law?

In groups

Discuss the statement below. Do you agree?

"Assisted suicide is too close to murder for the law to be able to distinguish clearly between them. The possibility of prosecution should continue to exist as a protection for the old and vulnerable against those who might wish them dead."
Alexander Chancellor, Journalist

Human cloning

Breakthrough in human cloning offers new transplant hope

Human cloning has been used to create stem cells for adults for the first time in a breakthrough which could lead to tissue and organs being regrown.

Using the cloning technique which produced Dolly the sheep in 1996, researchers were able for the first time to turn adult human skin cells into stem cells, which can grow into any type of tissue in the body.

The breakthrough could lead to new tissue-transplant operations for a range of debilitating disorders, such as Parkinson's disease, multiple sclerosis, heart disease and spinal cord injuries.

However, the breakthrough is likely to reignite the debate about the ethics of creating human embryos for medical purposes and the possible use of the same technique to produce cloned babies – which is illegal in Britain.

The author of the research admitted that without strong regulations the early embryos produced in therapeutic cloning "could also be used for human reproductive cloning, although this would be unsafe and grossly unethical".

There are two types of human cloning:

■ **Therapeutic cloning** involves the creation of human embryos that are used in scientific research and then destroyed. Organs for transplants could be created in this manner. Therapeutic cloning is legal in the UK.

■ **Reproductive cloning** would involve a cloned embryo being placed in a woman's womb and allowed to continue to develop into a baby. Reproductive cloning is possible in theory, but scientific research to achieve it in practice is not allowed in the UK.

Some people are opposed to both forms of human cloning, such as the Society for the Protection of the Unborn Child (SPUC):

"Human cloning for so-called therapeutic purposes is completely unethical. Such research creates life with the purpose of destroying it and therefore fails to respect the right to life of the human embryo. The human embryo in such circumstances is treated as resource material, rather than as a human individual with inherent dignity and fundamental human rights." SPUC

In groups

1 What is the difference between therapeutic cloning and reproductive cloning? Read the newspaper article and discuss the arguments for and against each type.

2 Organise a class debate to consider whether human cloning is right or wrong.

For your file

"All forms of human cloning should be banned."

Say why you agree or disagree with this statement.

Aim To improve your study skills, especially when revising for exams

Planning ahead

How good are you at managing your time or planning ahead at your studies? So much time is spent preparing for exams and completing coursework assignments, that it is important that you structure your time effectively.

Planning will help you break down your work into manageable tasks, and ensure that you don't leave everything to the last minute. Follow the tips (below) if you want to be an expert planner – it's one of the best and easiest ways of making sure your revision is really effective.

Top tips
for successful planning

1 **Set yourself targets.** These give you something to aim for and allow you a sense of achievement when you reach them.

2 **Think about all your goals.** Make sure that your goals are sufficient. They must ensure that you achieve what you want to do.

3 **Be realistic.** If you set yourself targets that you cannot achieve, you will set yourself up for failure and frustration.

4 **Be flexible.** Don't expect that you will be able to keep to your timetable without a hitch. Something is likely to crop up to upset your planning, so be prepared to make some late adjustments.

5 **Don't overplan.** This can be an excuse for not starting important work. If your original targets turn out to be unrealistic, you can always revise your work schedule later.

6 **Monitor your progress.** Check whether you are keeping up with your work schedule. Make any necessary adjustments if you fall behind.

LEARN ACTIVELY

How do you revise? Do you re-read your notes? Do you learn them by covering up the page and testing yourself? To help you distinguish the useful from the useless approaches, you need to spot the differences between the following two types of revision:

1 Passive revision – this involves trying to take information in without attempting to reproduce it in a new way. It will almost always let you down.

2 Active revision – this involves reproducing what you learn in some way, usually by condensing it. It engages your mind in a creative effort. The more creative, the more memorable. It's the best way to learn.

Examples of each type are given opposite.

In pairs

1 On your own, draw up a study planner for the next month using the advice on the left.

2 In pairs, look at each other's monthly study planners and discuss whether you think the goals set down are sufficient, realistic and flexible. Can you suggest ways in which your partner's study plan could be improved?

Active revision

✓ Writing index cards

Boiling down your material into key points that you can fit on index cards makes you think about what you are reading. It also makes your notes easy to refer back to.

✓ Annotating your texts

Making notes in the margins of your texts is an effort to understand their meaning. You have to work out what the passage is about, and put this into your own words.

✓ Mind mapping

This is a very effective and personal way to reproduce and understand your notes. Because it makes use of colour, drawing and space, mind mapping stimulates the creative side of the brain. It also makes information easy to record and recall.

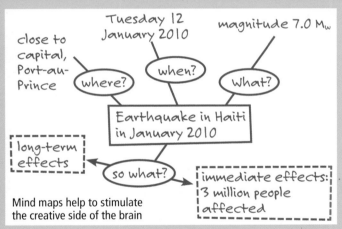

Mind maps help to stimulate the creative side of the brain

✓ Repeating out loud

Talking out loud is an excellent method of getting you to think creatively about something. Ask someone to test you, or simply talk to the wall. If you're trying to learn a list of things, repeating or chanting it over and over again really fixes it in your mind (remember doing times tables?).

✓ Doing past papers

When you're ready, try doing a past paper. This will force you to remember everything you need to know – or show up where you have to do further revision. It also makes you familiar with the way your exam papers are laid out, and the sort of questions that are asked.

Passive revision

✗ Rereading

Simply reading your notes over and over again doesn't engage the mind. It'll probably make you fall asleep instead. You take the information in, but do nothing with it to fix it in your mind.

✗ Copying out

This has the same problem – and, even worse, it takes forever. You'll find that your brain will be concentrating on getting the words down exactly right, rather than on anything more useful or creative.

✗ Putting your notes on computer

Another waste of time – see above. Why should you need your notes on computer? You're not getting them published.

✗ Highlighting

Highlighting key words and passages takes less time than the passive methods above, but you're only kidding yourself if you think this is a useful activity. It makes your notes look colourful, but does nothing to fix them in your mind.

Source: *The Student's Guide to Exam Success* by Eileen Tracy

In pairs

1 Are you an active or a passive reviser? Give reasons.

2 Which methods of revision work best for you? Should you change your approach, and if so, how?

For your file

Summarise the key points from the information above on active revision. Create a mind map of ways to improve your revision technique.

Coping with exams

Aim To explore strategies to use when preparing for and taking exams

Beat pre-exam stress

Stress can show up in lots of different ways. Tiredness, change in appetite, aches and pains, sleep problems, itching and rashes and feeling emotional are just a few. If you're really stressed you might also have panic attacks. Here are some great tips to help bust stress before an exam:

- Get plenty of sleep, eat a healthy diet and do lots of physical activities.

- Don't spend the whole time locked up with your books. Take regular breaks.

- Try not to feel guilty or anxious when you're not revising. Staying calm will help you remember what you revise and help you to perform better in an exam.

- In the exam you'll feel less stressed the more prepared you are, so start revising as early as you can.

Source: www.bbc.co.uk

Exams:
your strategy for success

PANIC! ...is a common response to the word 'exam'. To cope with this response, it is important to feel in control. You need a strategy.

Eight-point exam strategy

1 When is the exam? (Write it on your year planner.)

2 What kind of exam? (Essay or multichoice.)

3 How long is the exam?

4 How many questions?

5 Do all the questions have to be answered, or is there a choice?

6 How many questions have to be answered from each section?

7 Do all the questions carry an equal number of marks?

8 How long will it take to read the exam paper? (By knowing how long it will take to read, and allowing five minutes for proofreading at the end, you can work out how much time is left and how long you can spend on each question.)

Source: *Study Skills: A Pupil's Survival Guide*, by Christine Ostler

In groups

1 How do you feel as you approach an exam? Discuss your feelings with other members of the group.

2 Make a list of the points made in the article 'Beat pre-exam stress'. Do you use any other stress-busting methods that you can share with the group?

On your own

Read 'Exams – your strategy for succcess' and 'Exam survival'. Draw up a shortlist of the six most useful points. Be prepared to explain why you have selected those six points.

Exam survival

The day before

1 Check the contents of your pencil case (it must be see-through). Have you a back-up pen, geometry equipment, etc? Do you have fresh batteries in your calculator?
2 Double-check the time of the exam and where it will be.
3 Read through your revision notes, but don't work too late.
4 Get some fresh air: don't stay in all day.
5 Have an early night, even if you can't get to sleep straight away.

On the day

1 Get up in plenty of time.
2 Eat some breakfast, even if it is only dry toast!
3 Check that you have everything you need.
4 Get to the place of the exam in plenty of time.
5 Don't talk to students who are over-excited or depressed.
6 Go to the loo.

At the start of the exam

1 Listen to the instructions carefully.
2 Put your watch on the table to keep an eye on the time.
3 Read the instructions carefully.
4 If there is a choice, read all the questions first.
   - Put a ✓ against those you think you could tackle.
   - Put a ✗ against those you definitely couldn't answer.
   - Put a ? against those you are not sure about.
   - Decide which question to answer first. Choose the easiest.
5 If you are stuck and can't find a question you can answer, see if there is one with three or four short sections. You might be able to answer one or two of them, so you will pick up some marks.
6 If you are running out of time and can't get the last answer finished, make sure you have made a plan containing all the important points. You may pick up some extra marks.
7 Try to proofread at the end.

After the exam

- If you can avoid it, don't compare answers with your friends.
- If you are free, go and do something nice. You deserve it.

Source: *Study Skills: A Pupil's Survival Guide* by Christine Ostler

For your file

"I get so stressed by exams that during my mocks I couldn't sleep. And I always run out of time in an exam. What should I do?" Gus

Write a reply to Gus.

Answer the question!

One of the examiners' most common complaints is that a student hasn't answered the question. Usually this is because the student's answer contains irrelevant material. There are two good ways of avoiding this pitfall:

- Read the question carefully.
- Think about what aspect of the topic the examiner is asking you to write about.

For example, the exam question is 'Explain the causes of the Black Death'. The phrase 'Black Death' may release a torrent of interesting information, all ready-formed in the memory banks of your brain. However, unless your answer is focused on explaining 'the causes' of the Black Death, much of it will be irrelevant, and you will lose precious marks.

It's also important to look at the instruction words the exam question has used. For example, 'Outline the arguments for and against abortion' will require a different answer from 'Comment on the arguments for and against abortion'. The second question asks you to give your own opinion on the arguments, whereas the first question does not.

In pairs

The following instruction words often appear in exam questions: 'Compare and contrast', 'Evaluate', 'Analyse', 'Illustrate', 'Give an account of…'

Write down what you understand by these phrases and compare your answers with other pairs.

Aim To discuss attitudes to marriage and long-term commitment, and explore their implications (Personal wellbeing 3f)

Cohabiting

The structure of families has changed in the last few decades. Instead of getting married, many people are living together or cohabiting. Some cohabiting couples eventually get married, some continue in committed unmarried relationships, and some of them break up.

Why marry?

"It's a way of making a public commitment to your partner."

"Marriage gives you security in your relationship."

"Marriage is just a legal contract. You don't need it for anything else."

"I want children and it's important to me that I am married before I have them."

"What's the point of marriage these days, unless you are religious?"

"I am a Hindu. We take marriage very seriously in our family."

In groups

1 Discuss the different views about marriage given above. What are your own views?

2 Is cohabitation a good alternative to marriage? Is it a good way to 'test out' the relationship? What rights do people who cohabit have?

The myth of common law marriage

Many people (40% according to a survey in 2013) mistakenly believe that simply living together can give you the same rights as marriage. They believe that 'common law marriage' is a recognised legal status. They are wrong.

Others believe that by having a child together they acquire legal rights, whether married, civil partnered, or not. They too are mistaken.

Only couples who get married or register a civil partnership will acquire legal rights and responsibilities in relation to each other.

We often don't check out our rights because it seems unromantic, or even untrusting, to raise legal and financial issues about a relationship. But exploring the common 'what ifs' before difficulties arise, puts couples and families on a more secure footing.

The rights of unmarried fathers

When a married couple separate, both mother and father have parental responsibility (PR). PR gives a parent the right to be involved in major decisions about their child, such as to authorise medical treatment, and the right of access.

If they are unmarried, the mother has automatic rights regarding any children. But an unmarried father only has parental responsibility if he has jointly registered the child's birth, or if both partners have signed a Parental Responsibility Agreement. This can be done at any time and can also be ordered by a court.

Even if a father does not have parental responsibility, he is still equally responsible for the financial welfare of his children. He can be contacted by the Child Support Agency to provide financial support.

Source: adapted from www.divorceresource.co.uk

In pairs

Discuss what parental responsibility is and what the rights of married couples are. How do the rights of unmarried fathers differ from those of married fathers?

Prenuptial agreements

A prenuptial agreement is a legal document which a couple both sign, setting out how they will handle their finances when they marry.

As 42% of marriages end in divorce, more and more couples are signing prenuptial agreements.

> **"Prenuptial agreements are a good idea, because they protect the interests of both couples."**
>
> **"They are unromantic and suggest that the couple don't trust each other."**
>
> **"You never know what's going to happen in the future – prenuptial agreements are a form of insurance."**

In pairs

1 Discuss the pros and cons of prenuptial agreements. Would you be willing to sign one, if you were getting married?

2 The average age for first marriages in England and Wales in 2012 was 33 for men and 31 for women. In 1972 the average age was 26 for men and 23 for women. Discuss why more people are marrying later in life.

For your file

"We may live in a throwaway society today: if one car doesn't suit, the fashion is to change it for another. But sadly this principle is too often applied to a partner." Jill Curtis

Write a reply stating whether you agree or disagree. Justify your views.

Long-term relationships

Aim To explore what it means to make a long-term relationship work

Be a perfect partner

It's not easy; in fact, it's a lot of hard work. But it's worth the effort because usually the more you put into a relationship, the more you get out of it.

The key to a good relationship is mutual respect and good communication. You have to be able to talk to your partner. This means being brave enough to discuss issues that may be upsetting. If you have a problem, don't hold back. A problem that's bottled up can get out of proportion. Talking it through can ease the pressure and enable you both to find a solution.

If your partner raises doubts about your relationship, put yourself in their shoes. Imagine how you would feel if you were them. Don't leap in and make accusations, don't get upset, let them speak – even if this means hearing things you don't like. Perhaps they have a valid point about something, which you could try to sort out.

Feeling comfortable about talking means feeling good about yourself. You need self-esteem to feel assertive. Be as true to yourself as you can. Respect your own thoughts and opinions and be honest about them. Your partner will love you for who you are. Pretending to be something you're not won't work in the long term.

Just as you should be yourself, your partner should be, too. This inevitably means that you won't agree on everything and could end up having rows. Accept that your partner has a right to their own views. You don't have to agree with those views, but you should respect them. It takes compromise to make a relationship work.

Give and take is one thing, but there may be issues on which you're not willing to compromise. It's okay not to see eye to eye on everything. It would be boring if you did. Listen to your partner's ideas and try to see it from their angle. Not finding common ground doesn't mean your relationship is doomed.

Source: www.bbc.co.uk/radio1/onelife

In pairs

1 Read the article 'Be a perfect partner'. Discuss what it says about making a long-term relationship work.

2 Think about what is the key to a good relationship. Make a list of three key skills needed to make a relationship work and give a reason for each one.

The wedding planners

Think you know the facts about arranged marriages? Sanna Nasrullah sets you straight

▲ Do arranged marriages work better than love marriages?

Arranged marriages are practised mainly by Muslims, Hindus and Sikhs. The tradition began a long time ago. Parents used to get their children married off to a person of their choice because they believed it was a sin to go out with someone before getting married.

Some parents used to organise this when their children were very young. This was not because they wanted to get rid of them but because they knew that children start having feelings for the opposite sex at a young age. Nowadays most parents don't try to arrange marriages until their children are at least 16, and usually much older.

Arranged marriages often used to depend on how much money the groom earned. But that is not so important now because women are usually able to have their own careers rather than being full-time housewives.

The girl has the last word

I am a Muslim and many Muslim parents feel strongly that their children must have an arranged marriage. What people may not realise is that the girl always has the last word. (Or at least she's meant to.) If her parents pick out a boy for her, she gets to see him a few times and have dinner with him. If she does not get along with him or simply doesn't like him enough to want to marry him, then she is supposed to be able to say 'No'. Some girls do get forced into arranged marriages but that is not what Islam teaches.

I'm going to have an arranged marriage. I trust my mum to find me the right man because no one knows me better than she does. I think people should trust their parents. I have seen in my life that arranged marriages work better than love marriages.

I believe in fate

My cousin had an arranged marriage about seven years ago. She now has three kids and is pregnant with the fourth. She is very happy with her life, and she loves her husband very much. It may help an arranged marriage to be successful if the bride and groom are strongly religious, though whatever the religion, and however strong the belief, it could still work. I believe that God helps arranged marriages to work, and I believe in fate.

My cousin and her husband were made for each other. Then I look at all the people who have married out of love and how those marriages didn't last. Most of my aunties and my close family have had love marriages and most of them have not worked at all. I don't know why this is, it's just the way the world works.

I'm not saying that all arranged marriages work, or that they don't. I just think people should be more open-minded about it and not just focus on the age of the girl or assume it's to do with the wealth of the husband. That kind of thing does not happen any more.

In groups

1 Discuss what you have learned about arranged marriages.

2 How would you feel if your parents or guardians wanted you to have an arranged marriage?

3 Do you agree that 'arranged marriages can work better than love marriages'? What reasons could explain this?

For your file

Write a personal statement called: "Arranged marriages: my view."

Source: adapted from www.exposure.org.uk

Becoming a parent

Aim To explore the effect that becoming a parent has on a person's life, particularly in relation to teenage pregnancy

Teenage parents

Britain still tops the league of teenage pregnancies in Europe. What is the reality of being a teenage parent?

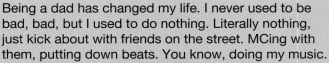

What it means to be a teenage mother

To say being a teenage mother is hard is an understatement. You've constantly got your baby to look after and many young mothers don't have a home of their own.

It's difficult even if the father stands by you. But the two girls that I know who are teenage mothers have to do it on their own, because the fathers didn't want to know. Even if the father is around, there's likely to be arguments because often they have to live with either the girl's or the boy's parents.

And there's the problem of money. Babies cost a lot to clothe and to feed.

One of the girls I know has kept on with her education and goes to college. But the other has dropped out.

It's hard for both of them. I don't know how I'd cope if I was in their position. Thank goodness I'm not.

Claire, 17

Charlie's Story

Charlie is 21 and has a two and a half year old son.

Being a dad has changed my life. I never used to be bad, bad, but I used to do nothing. Literally nothing, just kick about with friends on the street. MCing with them, putting down beats. You know, doing my music.

I used to sign on. That was the first thing I did when Tania found out she was pregnant. I had to get a job before I could tell my mum. I had to get a future. I knew she'd say that I had to be responsible now. I want to have a future. I want to be able to give my son what he wants. Not like a PS4 or anything, but so he can do what he wants to do.

There has to be a dad around to support the child. It's the dad that gives the discipline. Boys need role models. The ones without dads are the ones that are shooting people on the street. If you have a child then you have to be around. A mum can only teach so much. You need a dad to put you on the right track. You have to be responsible for a child for 18 years. If that means being unhappy for that time, then you have to do it. Me? I'm much happier now than I ever was before.

Source: *Young Foundation*

In groups

1 Discuss what Claire says about being a teenage mother. List all the things that can make life difficult for a teenage mother.

2 Talk about what Charlie says about being a dad. Why does he say a dad is important? Do you agree with what he says about the role of a father figure?

3 List all the things that change when you have a baby as a teenager – for the girl and for the boy. Should the boy always accept his responsibility and stay with the girl and support her? Give reasons for your view.

Sex education

"All young people have the right to good quality Sex and Relationships Education (SRE) which will help prepare them for adulthood. SRE should provide young people with accurate information on sex and sexuality, and help them to develop essential life skills, as well as a positive attitude to sexual and reproductive health." **Anna Martinez, Sex Education Forum**

"Young people in Britain are encouraged to regard sexual relations from an early age as desirable as long as they use contraception… The Government needs to be telling young people not to have sex yet, rather than telling them sex is fine but they need to be using contraception… Public policy should be reviewed to see if there are ways in which the traditional family, based on marriage, could be shored up rather than undermined." **Robert Whelan, Director of the Family Education Trust**

I want a baby

"I'll feel grown up and no one will be able to tell me what to do." Shona

"Maybe he'll stay with me if I have his baby." Hannah

"It's a way out. I won't have to get a job I don't like." Teresa

"Someone will love me." Gill

"I'll get money and my own flat from the council." Donna

"I want to feel better about myself." Jackie

"I'll have someone cute to love." Ruth

Source: www.thestraighttalkingproject.co.uk/why.html

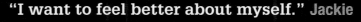

In pairs

1 Look at the reasons above given by teenage girls who want a baby. Discuss each reason in turn and decide whether you think it is a good reason for having a baby.

2 Imagine that a friend gives you one of the reasons above for trying for a baby. Write notes on what you would say to her, and be prepared to share them with the class.

In groups

Deciding to start a family is one of the most important decisions a couple can make.

1 Make a list of all the positive aspects of starting a family. Include all the pleasures that parenthood brings.

2 Make a list of all the reasons why you may not want to start a family. What responsibilities and problems does parenthood bring?

3 As a class, discuss whether your assessment would change depending on circumstances, such as your age when starting a family.

In pairs

Discuss the two different views held on sex education in Britain (above). Which do you think is the right approach? Which is more likely to reduce teenage pregnancy?

Parenthood

Aim To explore the roles and responsibilities of parents

Being a parent

Being a parent can be the most rewarding thing you ever do, and the toughest. This is because there are certain responsibilities that come with being a parent, and there are certain things that children need and that parents need to do.

Some of the qualities you need as a parent remain important all through your children's lives – above all, showing love and giving physical care. However, you have to show these qualities in different ways as your children grow up.

New baby

What your baby needs

Everything – a new baby is totally dependent on you to get what they need.

Patience and understanding – she can only tell you she is unhappy by crying and it takes time to work out what she wants.

Lots of attention – by responding to her cries and showing that you care when she's distressed, your baby will learn that she is loved.

What you need

Time for you, and your partner if you have one, to adjust to the changes a new baby brings.

Patience and understanding – the demands of a newborn can be emotionally and physically exhausting, especially during the first few weeks. As well as having no time to yourself, relationships can come under strain.

To look after yourself, as well as your baby – accept help from friends, family, neighbours.

Toddlers

What your toddler needs

To be able to develop her personality.

To learn about the world and discover what she can and what she can't do – this might seem like she is testing you all the time.

To be allowed to do as much as possible for herself.

To be encouraged and praised for any good behaviour, e.g. sharing.

To have set limits on behaviour, e.g. "Hitting hurts. Say it with words."

What you need

Time to recharge your batteries – this can be an exhausting and challenging time.

To spend time with your partner, if you have one. If you are on your own, try to find ways you can spend some time with grown-ups, so that you get some breaks from being alone with your child, e.g. join a parent and toddler group.

Source: *Parentline Plus*

How to be...
a 'good enough' parent

Forget trying to be the perfect parent – it's impossible. Try to be 'good enough', which means you'll need to show:

- **love, love, love** – a bottomless supply, especially in the first few years when you are building up your child's self-esteem. Love also means providing physical care – warmth, rest and nutritious meals.

- **self-sacrifice** – children need a huge amount of time and attention. This will mean making sacrifices, especially when they are very young.

- **consistency** – children like routines, and need to know what the ground rules are for behaviour. Consistent but not over-strict rules help them feel secure and allow you to manage behavioural problems.

- **listening skills** – always listen to what your children have to say. They deserve your attention and respect, and will grow in confidence if they are listened to.

- **a sense of humour** – especially at 4 a.m. when your four-year-old son wants to dress up as Batman for his party at midday, or when your teenage daughter phones late at night to ask for a lift home.

What is a mother?

She's the one we turn to
when we feel lost and sad,
she's our steadying anchor,
the best friend we've ever had.

She's the one who went without
to keep us clothed and fed,
the one who dried our tears,
and tucked us up in bed.

She's the one who understood
our childhood hopes and fears,
the one who praised our efforts
through all our growing years.

Source: *Smells of Childhood* by Mary M. Donoghue

What is a father?

"There is a difference between a father and a dad. A dad comes every now and then to give the mother money if the child needs anything. A father is there for his child whenever. He speaks to his child, advises his child, makes the child see the world. I see myself as a father, because my dad was a dad." **Richard, 19**

Source: *Babyfathers: New Images of Teenage Fatherhood* by Edmund Clark

In groups

1 Discuss what you have learned about being a parent. What skills and qualities do parents need to have in order to care for (a) a new baby and (b) a toddler?

2 Make a list of what children need:
(a) from ages 4 to 11
(b) during adolescence (12+).

In pairs

Read 'What is a mother?' and 'What is a father?' and discuss these questions:

1 Does Mary Donoghue give a realistic picture of what a mother is? Could you be this kind of mother? What does the poem leave out?

2 What was Richard's experience of his own father? Explain what kind of father he wants to be. Has he left anything out?

For your file

Write a paragraph explaining why you should aim to be a 'good enough' parent rather than a 'perfect' parent.

Aim To examine choices in education, work or training available after the end of Year 11

What are your options at 16?

There are lots of options available after Year 11. Do you want to stay on in the sixth form? Or move to a further education college? Do you want to start work as an apprentice? Or even start your own business? You have to make the decision that is right for you. You do not have to stay at school, but you have to continue with some form of education or training until you are 18. The chart shows the three choices you have.

END OF YEAR 11

CONTINUE FULL-TIME LEARNING

You can do a full-time course after Year 11 – either in the sixth form at school or by enrolling at a further education or specialist college. There are many different places you can study, and hundreds of different courses, so it is important that you find out about both the place and the course you are thinking of studying.

Some levels of course are suited to different skills. These can be divided into **general courses** and **vocational courses**, although there are also some mixed programme courses.

General courses are not geared towards a specific career path – A levels in History, English or Chemistry are examples. However, this does not mean that you are less likely to get a job later on – it keeps your options open. For some career paths, though, you will need to choose certain subjects to study.

On a **vocational course** you study and gain skills in a particular career area. For example, you might take a BTEC in something like Health and Social Care or Business Studies. Vocational courses point you in the direction of particular careers.

START WORK-BASED TRAINING

Work-based training is when you learn new skills and a profession in the workplace rather than in a school classroom.

For example, you could start your working life as an apprentice, beginning at the level that suits you best. This gives you the opportunity to gain an NVQ (National Vocational Qualification) or similar qualification – the level depends on your own ability.

In some schemes, for example Life Skills, you can sample different jobs for short periods of time. Other schemes, such as the Entry to Employment (E2E) programme, help if you want to start work but are not yet ready to cope on your own.

FIND A JOB AND CONTINUE EDUCATION PART TIME

Find a job or do volunteering for more than 20 hours a week, and continue with part-time education leading to an accredited qualification. Although you may be keen to start earning money it is vital that you think about what skills you can develop and what qualifications you can obtain.

HIGHER EDUCATION

QUALIFICATIONS

FULL-TIME EMPLOYMENT

Going to college

Case study: Kay

Kay wanted a change from her previous educational experience and chose Newcastle College because the course appealed to her more than staying at school. Studying at the college allows Kay to set her own goals and targets that are preparing her for adult life.

The science course offers students the opportunity to work within a laboratory environment, with students taking part in various experiments. Kay has worked her way up from basic experiments within chemistry, physics and biology to more advanced lab work.

"The facilities for genetics and microbiology are excellent and there's always free equipment on hand. Being able to work within this environment has really helped boost my confidence."

In pairs

1 Discuss what you have learned about some of the different options that are available at the end of Year 11.

2 Draw up a list of advantages for each of the main options given in the flowchart (left): continuing in full-time learning; starting work-based training; and getting a job. What disadvantages are there?

For your file

1 Write a personal statement describing what choices attract you after Year 11. Give reasons for your statements and don't be afraid to express doubts or uncertainties.

2 "You don't need any qualifications these days." Jennifer
Write a reply to Jennifer.

College courses

Most colleges offer a range of courses at different levels. The entry requirements for a course depend on the level of the course.

- **Level 1 courses.** These are basic courses providing an introduction to a subject, industry or area of work. They lead to qualifications such as NVQ level 1 and the BTEC Introductory Certificate. These are roughly equivalent to GCSE grades D–G.

- **Level 2 courses.** These provide a deeper understanding of a subject or area of work, leading to qualifications such as NVQ level 2 and the BTEC First Diploma. They are roughly equivalent to GCSE grades A–C. Many employers like young people to have a level 2 qualification as a minimum.

- **Level 3 courses.** These lead to qualifications such as A levels, NVQ level 3 and the BTEC National Diploma. This level is almost always needed for entry to university and employers will look for this level of qualification for applicants for many jobs.

- **Vocational qualifications.** National Vocational Qualifications (NVQs) are work-based awards, available in a huge variety of careers. They are delivered either in the workplace or somewhere set up to be like a workplace.

- **BTECS.** These are general vocational qualifications, available in subjects linked to an area of work, such as engineering, art and design and business studies, combining practical work with academic learning. Both NVQs and BTECs can lead either to employment or further study.

Source: *adapted from Newcastle College website, www.ncl-coll.ac.uk*

What are apprenticeships?

Aim To explain what apprenticeships and traineeships are and what they offer young people

An apprenticeship is a real job with training, so you can earn while you learn and pick up nationally recognised qualifications as you go. Apprenticeships take from one to four years to complete and cover 1500 job roles in a wide range of industries from things like engineering to finance advice, veterinary nursing to accountancy.

Key benefits

- Earning while you learn.
- Training in the skills employers want.
- Excellent progression opportunities, whether looking to study further or climb the ranks within the workplace.
- Increased future earning potential. Apprentices enjoy marked salary increases when they complete their training.
- Better long-term salary prospects.

Source: www.apprenticeships.org.uk

Case study: Ikrah

Ikrah was recruited as a Business Administration Apprentice for Rotherham Metropolitan Borough Council on leaving school, enabling her to develop an early insight into a business environment.

When asked about her time as an apprentice Ikrah said, "I struggled at first to get used to the difference between being at school and a busy office environment but people were patient and supportive so I quickly picked up new skills and got into the work routine."

Ikrah attended college for half a day per week as part of her apprenticeship in order to study for a level 2 in Business Administration.

After completing the apprenticeship Ikrah got a permanent job as a Business Administration Assistant with the Council. She a said, "I would recommend being an apprentice to anyone as you get to learn and gain experience at the same time."

Source: adapted from Rotherham College website, www.rotherham.ac.uk

Traineeships

Traineeships are courses for people who are not quite ready to do an apprenticeship. The courses provide the opportunity for you to gain experience in an area of employment in which you are interested.

A traineeship increases your chances of getting a job by focusing on developing the basic skills which employers are looking for. At the end of your work experience you will be given a reference and an interview if there is a job available.

Placement opportunities are available across a wide range of industries, and students who complete a traineeship are better prepared for employment or an apprenticeship.

Case study: Wilson

What do you do if you are unsure which career path to follow but want to get some practical experience? For Wilson Borromeo, this was a pressing concern as he was unhappy with the theoretical nature of his motor mechanic course and wondered if IT might suit him better.

He was offered a traineeship by Nationwide Computer Services, which provides a range of IT services including repairs, virus removal and data recovery.

Over a four-month period, Wilson gained a string of qualifications and great first-hand experience working closely with IT technicians.

The traineeship not only enabled him to pick up relevant technical skills, but also improved his presentation skills. When it ended, he was immediately offered an apprenticeship by another firm.

Source: adapted from Barnet Southgate College website, www.barnetsouthgate.ac.uk

Should I go to Sixth Form or College?

Derek Stuart says: It's your choice.

In many areas of the country there are schools with their own sixth forms offering courses to follow on from your GCSEs. Some areas have a sixth-form college to which you can apply.

In all areas, there are also colleges which often provide a much wider range of courses than most schools can offer.

Whether you choose to stay on at school may be determined by what results you get in your GCSEs and by what subjects or course you want to take.

There are other factors you will want to consider, such as how far you will have to travel.

More importantly, think about your interests. Collect as much information as you can about courses and possible careers. Talk to people – at school, at college and at home.

Don't let others make up your mind for you. It's your choice.

In groups

Discuss the courses you are considering doing. Say why you are thinking of staying on at school or going to college to continue your education and training.

For your file

Explain what you have learned from these pages about apprenticeships and traineeships.

Applying for jobs

Aim To understand what makes a good job application form and CV, and how to prepare for an interview

Job applications

Applying for a job may seem a daunting thing to do, but if you take care over your application, and follow a few simple rules, you will improve your chances. There are usually three different ways in which you can be asked to present yourself:

1 APPLICATION FORMS

An application form will ask you to give facts about yourself, and to list your experience, activities and interests.

You may be asked to write a paragraph saying why you are applying for that particular vacancy, and what skills you think you can bring to the job.

It's a good idea to use a black pen when filling out the form, and to practise completing a photocopy of the form first.

3 CVs

Most employers will ask you to send a CV when applying for a job. A CV is a brief summary of the important facts about yourself and your experience. You can keep it on your computer and adapt it to send to many prospective employers.

A traditional CV lists, in date order, your education, qualifications and work experience. However, you may want to write a 'skills-based' CV (see example opposite) if you feel your skills are more relevant than your qualifications.

2 LETTERS OF APPLICATION

Some employers may ask you to put information about yourself in a letter of application. The key things to remember are to:

- keep the letter short – no more than two sheets of paper
- include your address and phone number
- state the title of the job you are applying for, and where you heard about it
- explain why you are interested in this job, and give details of any related work experience you have
- give contact details for any referees who have agreed to provide references for you
- write the letter out in rough first and then get someone to check the spelling and grammar.

Source: *16 and Beyond* © Hereford and Worcester Careers Service 200

For your file

Write your own CV – it can be either a traditional or a 'skills-based' CV.

In pairs

1 Your teacher will give you a job advert. Discuss how you would write a letter of application.

2 Draft your own letter of application and then comment on your partner's draft, suggesting ways in which they could improve it.

3 Produce a final copy of your letter of application on your own.

Example of a 'skills-based' CV

If you have a record of achievement, use it to help you develop your personal employability skills section.

GRAHAM JONES
22 Lower Grange Road, Newtown NT4 6HQ
Telephone: 0777 9123687 (mobile)
Email: JonesG20@Smartconnect.co.uk
Date of birth: 13.04.94

Include personal details. There is no need to write CV at the top.

Personal skills
- Excellent practical skills, skilled at working with metal and mending things.
- Punctual and reliable.
- Capable and hard worker.
- Good communicator, able to talk to people of all ages.
- Keen to train and gain motor vehicle qualifications.

Education
2005–2010 Newtown Academy.
Predicted to achieve GCSE grades D–E in Technology and Maths.

List secondary schools or colleges attended.

If you haven't done much work experience, think about your hobbies and interests. Are any of the personal skills you have developed relevant to the job?

Work and other relevant experience
- June 2009: in Year 10, completed two weeks' work experience placement at Smart Cars Garage, Weston Road, Newtown. Helped the mechanics strip down an engine, replace a gear box and clean up.
- Able to maintain and repair own BMX.

One referee should be from your school/ college. Ask your referees for their permission first.

References

Mr H Brake (Manager)
Smart Cars Garage
Weston Road,
Newtown NT4 5BB
HandDBrake@Quik.com

Mrs B Temper
Newtown Academy
Cresington Drive
Newtown NT4 8NW
BDTemper@NTA.sch.uk

- Make it look good.
- Check all the details and spelling.
- Keep it short – two pages at the most.

Source: www.courses-careers.com magazine

Preparing for your interview

"Aargh! The dreaded interview! What if they don't like me! What if I make a fool of myself?"

Relax! You will be amazed how many people feel like this, particularly when they are inexperienced at interviews. Here are some top tips to help:

- **Be polite**
- **Dress smartly**
- **Be positive**
- **Be confident**
- **Don't be afraid to ask questions**
- **Be interested**
- **Do your research – be informed.**

In pairs

1 Read the top tips on the left and discuss why they are important. What other tips would you give someone preparing for an interview? Draw up a list of five more tips, then compare them with another pair's list.

2 Choose a job or college course that you are interested in. Draw up a list of questions that you could be asked and role-play the interviews, for example:

"Why do you want to come to this college?"

"Why do you think this course suitable is for you?"

"What appeals to you about this job?"

"What qualities do you have to offer this company?"

"What do you think are your strengths and weaknesses?"

For your file

Write an advice leaflet on one of the following:
- writing a job application letter
- writing a CV
- preparing for an interview.

Aim To explore human rights issues, focusing on cases of human rights abuses and looking at how human rights can be protected and enforced

Protecting human rights

A key way to protect human rights is to educate people. Once people know their rights, they can complain when they are being violated. The Universal Declaration of Human Rights argues that 'all people should be free to fulfil their potential'.

▲ Can torture ever be justified?

Raising awareness

Raising awareness of human rights abuses is another way to protect human rights. Some pressure groups send human rights observers to conflict areas where human rights are being abused. International observers can often protect human rights just by their very presence.

Observers can also be sent to a country where an election is being held to ensure voters' rights to freedom of expression.

Letting governments know that human rights abuses are being noted can act as a very useful deterrent. The most successful example of this is the 'Prisoner of Conscience' Campaign run by Amnesty International. This pressure group encourages people to write to governments holding prisoners who have committed no real crime and whose human rights are being abused. Sometimes the prisoners are set free, sometimes not.

Pressure groups, such as Liberty, work to promote human rights and civil liberties by supporting test cases in the courts, by lobbying and by campaigning. Liberty's campaigns range from defending privacy to condemning torture and protecting free speech.

In pairs

What do you think is the most effective way of protecting human rights? Why?

Strengthening the law

Stronger laws mean greater legal protection. This is one reason why the EU has drafted the European Charter of Fundamental Rights. One of the new protections it offers is a ban on financial gain from the human body. This strengthens the law against slavery, illegal organ transplants and the selling of surrogate babies, and it may strengthen the law against prostitution.

On your own

Find out about Amnesty International's Youth Urgent Action Network, which provides monthly alerts to protect people in danger, by visiting www.amnesty.org.uk. Read the latest case details and choose which action to take.

Enforcing human rights internationally

Sometimes governments ignore human rights. For example, in Bosnia in the 1990s the government pursued a policy of 'ethnic cleansing' – forcing people from one ethnic group to move out of their homes or killing them.

When protecting human rights fails, enforcement becomes necessary. This can involve prosecuting war criminals or, in extreme cases, direct military intervention and regime change.

Former Bosnian Serb leader Radovan Karadzic appeared at the UN Yugoslav war crimes tribunal in The Hague, Netherlands.

The International Criminal Court

The International Criminal Court (ICC) was set up in 2002 and is based at The Hague in the Netherlands. The idea is that it doesn't matter where the criminal committed the crime: if it was illegal under international law they will be prosecuted.

For example, in October 2009 the trial started of Radovan Karadzic who led the Bosnian Serbs into a war between 1992 and 1995 in which 100,000 people died. He faced 11 counts of war crimes, including two of genocide, over the 43-month siege of Sarajevo and the 1995 massacre of 8000 Muslim men and boys at Srebrenica.

Although 60 countries have signed the treaty recognising the ICC, the USA has refused to do so. The USA says it will not have its soldiers subject to the international rules of an external court. The USA believes this would limit what they could do to intervene and protect human rights. Critics of the USA say if it wants to improve human rights around the world, it has to be subject to the same rules as everyone else.

Military intervention and regime change

Sometimes, in the case of widespread human rights abuses, only the use of force will prevent further abuses from occurring. This has led countries to use military intervention to stop human rights abuses.

The most extreme example of military intervention is regime change, such as the US-led invasions of Afghanistan in 2001, which removed the Taliban from power, and of Iraq in 2003 which brought about the downfall of the dictator Saddam Hussein.

The aim in Afghanistan was to replace the Taliban government, which was sheltering Al-Qaeda terrorists. This was quickly achieved. But US and British troops remained in Afghanistan until 2014. The UK government argued that the troops were protecting national security by preventing the Taliban from regaining power, which would lead to Afghanistan once again becoming a base for terrorism. In addition, the government was protecting the rights of Afghan citizens e.g. women who would be denied an education by a Taliban government.

In groups

"If, in order to protect the human rights of the majority, it means violating the human rights of a few people, then that's acceptable." Jonas

"Military intervention is fine, but regime change isn't. Everyone has the right to self-determination." Mary

Look at the statements above. Do you agree or disagree with them? Why? Give reasons for your views.

For your file

Write a statement saying whether you think Britain was right to take part in the initial invasion of Afghanistan in 2001, and whether British troops should have been withdrawn once regime change was achieved.

Human rights abuse

Aim To explore human rights issues and to examine cases of human rights abuse

Basic survival needs

Basic necessities are those things that we cannot do without. These include food, clean water, shelter and clothing. These necessities are meant to be protected by Article 25 of the Universal Declaration of Human Rights, which states that:

"Everyone has the right to an adequate standard of living, including food, clothing, housing, and medical care."

Despite this, basic necessities are not met for different people across many parts of the world.

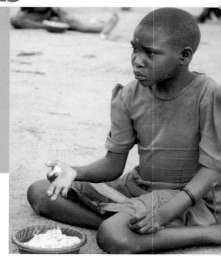

▲ Children have the right to have enough food to survive

Human rights abuses

International human rights problems are not just confined to necessities. Human rights pressure groups have identified a long list of human rights abuses that occur around the world. Among the most common rights violated are the following:

Rights violated	How
The right to fair employment	• In India, moneylenders often exploit workers by charging them high interest on loans that they can never pay back. As a result, many workers end up in 'debt slavery', saving virtually no money from their work because so much goes back to the moneylender.
The right to be presumed innocent until proven guilty	• In France the reverse applies. If you are charged with a crime, the responsibility is on you to prove you are innocent. The French claim that their legal system still works, but critics say that it is unfair.
The right to live in safety and security	• As a result of the ongoing conflict in Israel, Jews and Palestinians live in constant fear of suicide bombings, assassinations, army retaliations, and civil unrest.
The right to freedom of speech	• People should be able to say what they like. In 2015, two terrorists killed twelve people in Paris, because the magazine *Charlie Hebdo* had published cartoons of the prophet Muhammad.
The right to life	• Although the USA is a signatory to the Universal Declaration of Human Rights, many states in the USA still have the death penalty.

"Basic necessities are more important than any other human rights. We should be concentrating on providing food and water where they are needed." Zara

"All human rights are equally important. What's the use of food and water if you can't live in safety and security?" Hamil

In groups

1 Discuss the statements on the left. Which do you agree with?

2 Make a list of the ten human rights you think are the most important. Put them in order of importance, then compare your views.

China's human rights record

- Death penalty – China executes more people each year than the rest of the world put together. One estimate puts the number at 8000 per year.
- Internet censorship – Censorship of the Internet continues with few signs that the authorities are prepared to relax surveillance and control.
- Re-education through labour – Critics of the government and members of banned religions can be sent to a labour camp for up to four years, without charge or trial.
- Torture – Torture is widespread in the criminal justice system – common methods include electric shocks, beating and sleep deprivation.
- Human rights defenders – People who make a stand are harassed and arrested, often relating to vague charges like 'state secrets'. They include lawyers, journalists, HIV activists and trade unionists.
- Religious persecution – Unofficial religious groups – such as the Falan Gong spiritual movement – are banned as 'subversive' and individual practitioners detained.

Source: www.amnesty.org.uk

India – The caste system

In India the caste system has deep roots, based on the Hindu belief that you are born into a certain class and cannot change. The lowest class is the Dalits (or 'Untouchables') who make up about 16% of India's population.

Discrimination against Dalits is outlawed, but is deeply ingrained. Many Dalits do not have their human rights respected and can do only the most menial jobs, such as stone breaking, clothes washing and sewer cleaning. They are made to live in colonies or slums outside villages and towns and denied proper housing, health care and education.

In groups

Discuss the statements below, saying why you agree or disagree with them.

"It is a state's responsibility to control what information is available to its citizens on the Internet. To deny access to certain sites is not an abuse of human rights."

"The use of torture can never be justified."

"Everyone has the right to life whatever they may have done. Executions are a violation of that right."

"In the interests of national security it may be necessary to detain someone without trial. The safety of a nation's citizens must come before the rights of the individual."

Role play

Search the Internet to find out more about the Dalits and how they have been treated over the centuries. Then role-play a scene in which a reporter interviews a Dalit family.

For your file

Minority ethnic or religious groups are often the victims of human rights abuses. Search the Internet to find examples, then focus on one group and draft a report to present to the class about their treatment.

Refugees, asylum seekers and economic migrants

Refugees and asylum seekers

Aim To understand the reasons why people become refugees and asylum seekers and to explore issues concerning their human rights

Human rights abuses can force people to leave the country in which they live and become refugees.

Many flee because of wars. Others leave because they are persecuted for their religion or political beliefs, or because they belong to a minority ethnic group and they are in danger of being arrested, tortured or killed.

At the end of 2013, there were 16.7 million refugees worldwide. The country with the largest number of refugees was Pakistan. There were also about 33.3 million people who were forced to leave their homes and were displaced within their own country. They are known as internally displaced people.

Countries with vast numbers of displaced people in 2013 were Syria (6.5 million), Colombia (5.4 million) and the Democratic Republic of Congo (almost 3 million).

Refugees can seek asylum in another country. If they are granted asylum, they have the right to be protected by the law of that country.

Many asylum seekers settle in the country that gives them asylum, because they are unwilling or afraid to return to their home country. However, only about 12 countries are prepared to offer some refugees a permanent home. Since 2005, people who are recognised as refugees are given permission to stay in Britain for only five years.

▲ Syrian refugees

In groups

What would life be like in a refugee camp? How would it be different from living in a city? Think about housing conditions, sources of food, water and energy for cooking, about education and school facilities, and about leisure activities. What things would you miss most about not living in your own country?

In pairs

"I think people feel it's part of what it means to be British to offer sanctuary to those who are being persecuted, tortured, subjected to violence, or fleeing conflict or famine. I think we are a tolerant and open-hearted nation and I feel that the best way to express that is to say to those who are really suffering, 'If you have no other options left, we will offer you sanctuary'."

Nick Clegg became Deputy Prime Minister in 2010

Why do people become refugees? Do you agree with Nick Clegg's view?

How many refugees are there?

- The UK refugee population was 126,055 in 2013 – approximately 0.23% of the UK population.

- Over 86% of the world's refugees are in less economically developed countries.

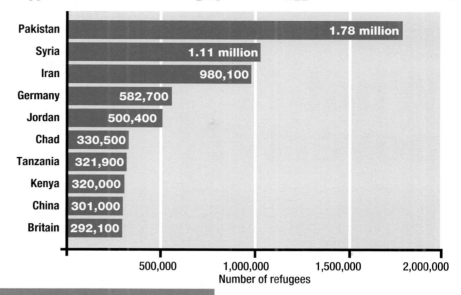

Country	Number of refugees
Pakistan	1.78 million
Syria	1.11 million
Iran	980,100
Germany	582,700
Jordan	500,400
Chad	330,500
Tanzania	321,900
Kenya	320,000
China	301,000
Britain	292,100

Number of refugees

Economic migrants and human trafficking

- About 21,500 people annually apply for asylum in the UK. Approximately two-thirds of these applications are refused initially. At present, asylum seekers whose applications fail are usually allowed to remain in the UK until their appeal against refusal has been heard. Only then, if their appeal fails, will they be deported.

- Although the number of asylum applications has fallen in recent years, there are concerns that the system of asylum is being exploited by people who simply wish to move to another country in order to improve their standard of living. These people are known as 'economic migrants'.

- Economic migrants could be anyone: a Polish plumber, a Portuguese agricultural worker, or an African nurse. They may be in the UK legally or illegally, depending on how they entered the country, and they may have a legal work permit or be working illegally.

- Some people see economic migrants as a threat, because they are regarded as taking jobs away from British-born people. Others view them as making a vital contribution to certain sections of the economy and the public services. For example, many jobs in the hotel and catering industry that are shunned by local workers are done by migrant workers. Many doctors and nurses in the NHS come from outside the UK.

- Economic migration has led to an increase in the crime of human trafficking. Criminal gangs lure people in less developed countries with promises of good jobs and a better life in a more developed country. They then smuggle these people into countries like the UK. Because these people cannot work legally, they are often forced to work for the criminal gangs, i.e. as prostitutes or as slave labour for little or no money.

In pairs

Which of the statements below do you agree with? Why? Give reasons for your views.

"If letting in three asylum seekers saves one person from persecution abroad, it's a price worth paying." Dominic

"People are just coming over here and taking advantage of those of us who were born in the UK." Abdul

"I'd rather have people here working legitimately than have them being exploited by criminal gangs." Lucy

For your file

Write a short article on 'economic migration' for an encyclopedia aimed at teenagers. You will need to explain clearly what it is, why it exists, and present some ways in which you feel it could be controlled.

Poverty

What is poverty?

Aim To define poverty and to examine how it could be eradicated

Poverty is a lack of money and possessions so severe that people cannot meet their basic needs. A person is living in real poverty when they cannot meet the basic needs for survival: water, food, clothing and shelter. Real poverty is a major problem in less economically developed countries in much of Africa and Asia.

Poverty in less economically developed countries

Over 80% of the world's population live in developing countries. These people earn less than 20% of the world's income. This leads to widespread real poverty. In 2008, the World Bank estimated that 1.4 billion people lived on less than $1.25 per day.

Many people have trouble meeting their basic needs for survival. For example, one consequence of real poverty in less developed countries is that they do not have the money to build proper water and sewage systems. This means that their standard of health is much lower. Famine and drought have plagued countries like the Sudan and Ethiopia for the last 30 years. This has made real poverty worse.

There is also relative poverty in less-developed countries. Often, there is a small wealthy elite in these countries. Alongside them is an underclass who live in absolute poverty. These people earn and own almost nothing. Buying a fridge would be unthinkable – they wouldn't be able to afford it. It is estimated that about 3 billion people live on less than $2.50 a day.

Poverty in more economically developed countries

'Relative poverty' describes how one group of people's standard of living compares to another's. In the UK, 1 in 4 children are said to live below the poverty line. The poverty line is the amount of money that is necessary for a basic standard of living. Thus while the vast majority of people may be able to meet their basic needs, their quality of life may be very low. Such relative poverty can be a major cause of crime, as people want the goods and lifestyle that more wealthy people enjoy in the same country.

In groups

Imagine you have only £5 per day to live on. What would you spend it on? What would you be short of?

In pairs

Imagine you lived life without the following items – a fridge, a cooker or a washing machine. What would life be like? How would it affect you? What would your life be like without an electricity supply or a clean water supply?

Eradicating poverty

What causes poverty?

Poverty is often the result of a number of factors such as:

- unfair trade
- wars and internal conflicts
- climate change
- lack of education and health facilities
- corrupt governments
- natural disasters.

"Greed and corruption are the greatest cause. India can afford nuclear weapons and a space programme, yet many of its people live in poverty in slums."

"Policies of governments and companies are keeping people poor. Policies that ensure that global trade benefits the rich, not the poor – the three richest men in the world are wealthier than the 48 poorest countries combined. Policies that give increasing power to multinational companies – for every £1 of aid going into poor countries, multinationals take 66p of profits out. The powerful are exploiting the poor to make bigger and bigger profits."

World Development Movement

Three actions that would end poverty

Improve access to education and health services

Education is the key to lifting many people out of poverty. In addition to opening up job opportunities, it makes young women, in particular, aware of health needs. Providing access to reproductive health services reduces the number of children born to poor families, and assists in reducing the spread of AIDS.

Make international trade fairer

Unfair trade rules, designed largely by rich countries, work against the interests of poor communities in developing countries. For example, the EU's economic partnership agreements with former colonies insist that they open up their markets to EU products, which can have a disastrous effect on local producers.

Increase aid to poorer countries

Donor countries need to deliver an increased $50 billion a year. This needs to be targeted at poor people's needs, in particular for basic healthcare and education. Aid should be made more effective by supporting poorer countries' own plans for development. It should not be conditional on the recipient countries having to promise to make economic changes.

Case study

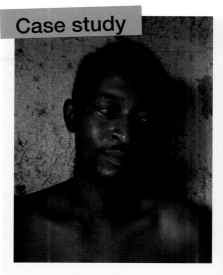

Kofi Eliasa used to own a tomato farm, but now he breaks stones in a quarry for a living, earning less than a dollar a day to feed his family.

He is one of the many farmers in Ghana who have fallen victim to cheap European food imports that have flooded the country ever since the Ghanaian government was forced to open up its markets in return for loans and aid from the International Monetary Fund (IMF) and the World Bank.

For your file

"It's up to the politicians to take action to end poverty. There's nothing I can do."

Say why you agree or disagree with this statement.

In pairs

1 What do you think are the main causes of world poverty? Which of the three actions suggested in the article do you think would be most effective in reducing poverty?

2 Plan a 30-second TV advert for a charity campaign 'End Poverty Now'. What is the main message you would want to get across?

Aim To understand what life expectancy is and the causes of ill health in the world

Life expectancy

Over the last 65 years, life expectancy has increased dramatically. In 1950 the average life expectancy was 46 years worldwide. Today it is over 70. This increase has been due to advances in medicine and improved living conditions.

In the more economically developed countries life expectancy is over 79. In Japan it is 83. In less economically developed countries life expectancy is lower. However, in most countries it is now 50 or over, with only Sierra Leone, the Central African Republic and the Democratic Republic of Congo being below 50.

The difference between the less developed countries and the more developed countries was highlighted by the Ebola epidemic in 2014. Countries in Africa were far less able to prevent the disease spreading than European and North American countries.

In pairs

List the reasons why you think there is a low life expectancy in so many African countries. Then compare your views.

The causes of ill health

Ill health is usually caused by environmental factors. This includes water pollution, diet, and working conditions. The World Health Organisation has estimated that up to 80% of all sickness and disease in less developed countries is caused by unsafe water and/or inadequate sanitation. This figure is set to rise due to global warming, as more freshwater areas become contaminated by salt in seawater.

Recent medical studies have suggested that up to 85% of cancer cases in more developed countries are caused by environmental factors. Meanwhile, heart disease, one of the biggest killers, is caused by a diet of too much fatty food, alcohol and smoking. Campaigners argue that to improve world health, we need to tackle its root causes. This includes our environment, and what we eat, drink and breathe.

Mental illness also causes widespread problems across the world. This results in deaths from stress, as people work longer hours in more stressful jobs. The World Health Organisation estimates that one in four of the world's population will experience some form of mental illness, such as stress or depression, in their lives. In addition, it is estimated that one in 20 people die due to stress in the long run.

Sanitation: THE FACTS

- **2.5 billion people do not have somewhere private, safe and hygienic to go to the toilet.**

- **The simple act of washing hands with soap and water after going to the toilet can reduce diarrhoea diseases by over 40%.**

- **Safe disposal of children's faeces leads to a reduction of nearly 40% in childhood diarrhoea.**

Source: www.wateraid.org.uk

Preventing diseases

A major factor in combating ill health has been immunisation. This involves giving people an injection to make them immune to a particular disease. Immunisation has actually led to one infectious disease, smallpox, being wiped out. The strength of immunisation is that it relies on prevention rather than a cure.

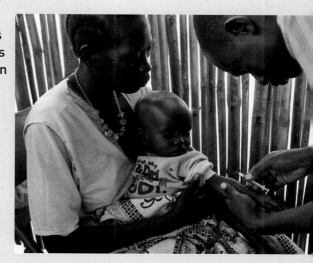

In 1974, only 5% of the child population of the world had been immunised against many common diseases. The World Health Organisation decided to target six of these diseases – measles, tuberculosis, smallpox, tetanus, whooping cough and diphtheria – and immunise people against them. A target of 80% of the world's population being immunised was met in 1990, and a target of 90% immunisation was partially met in 2000. However, in the 25 least developed countries, only 50% of children have been immunised.

Ebola

At present, there is no vaccine available to immunise people against Ebola. There was an outbreak of Ebola in West Africa in 2014. The countries most affected were Guinea, Sierra Leone and Liberia, three of the poorest countries, with weak health systems and poor sanitation in many cities. The World Health Organisation declared an emergency and clinics were hastily built in order to try to stop the disease from spreading.

The overuse of antibiotics

Antibiotics are drugs prescribed by doctors to treat infections caused by bacteria. While antibiotics are still effective against many bacteria, a major problem is that some bacteria have appeared that are resistant to antibiotics. This is particularly a problem in hospitals, where new infections, like MRSA and C.Difficile have evolved, which are immune to most antibiotics. This has led the NHS to order doctors to prescribe antibiotics only when they are strictly necessary.

One particular global problem is malaria, which is a threat to 45% of the world's population. Antibiotic-resistant strains, coupled with global warming, mean that 60% of the world's population may be threatened by malaria by 2050.

Education

Aim To understand the different levels of education around the world, and the barriers to education that exist

Levels of education

Levels of education vary widely across the world. In some developed countries, the literacy rate – the number of people who can read and write – is as high as 100%, for example in Finland and Norway. In the United Kingdom it is 99%. However, in less developed countries, it is much lower. In Niger only 15% can read and in Burkina Faso only about one in five people can read.

In 2012, 91% of children in the world were enrolled in school. Although the number of children of primary age not in school has declined from 100 million in 2000 to 58 million in 2012, the aim of universal primary education by 2015 is unlikely to be met. The lowest rates of school participation are in Western and Central Africa and South Asia.

In many countries, poorer children are less likely to go to school and children in rural areas are twice as likely not to attend school as children in urban areas. Girls, too, are at a disadvantage in some countries, particularly in Africa, the Middle East and South Asia.

Education and poverty – a vicious circle

Education and poverty are closely related. In many less economically developed countries people move to cities to find work. However, without a formal education, many cannot find a job. This often forces them into dwellings on the edge of cities without a clean water supply or sanitation. Without adequate health education, they do not fully understand the risks of living in such shanty towns.

Poverty also causes a lack of education. Without resources, schools cannot be built, teachers cannot be paid and transport to school cannot be provided.

The result is a vicious circle. Without providing education, a country cannot climb out of poverty; while poverty still exists, there are no resources available to develop its education system.

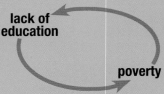

lack of education

poverty

In groups

Imagine what it would be like to have only attended primary school, but not secondary school. What would you have missed out on? Now imagine only having one year at school. What would you have learned? What effect would this have on the rest of your life?

In pairs

Use the Internet to find out what charities such as Oxfam are doing to help LEDCs to provide education for their children, and what pressure groups such as the Global Campaign for Education are doing. Research how your school can get involved with the next Global Action Week (www.campaignforeducation.org).

Less economically developed countries
– the barriers to education

In less economically developed countries, there are many barriers to education.

Firstly, there can be a lack of educational resources. No books, no Internet, no pens, and no pencils. Children can sometimes be taught in classes of 60 or more, leading to little contact time with teachers. Asking questions can be nearly impossible.

In addition, there may be other things that provide a barrier to education. Children may be forced to work, to help provide for their families. In 2014 there were 168 million children working as child labourers, mainly in agriculture. Over 20% of the children in sub-Saharan Africa were working.

Older children may be caring for younger children in the family, if the mother has to go and work. In war zones, children may be forced to fight in conflicts as child soldiers, putting their lives at risk and emotionally scarring them for many years. Girls may be denied access to education and forced to stay at home by religious extremists.

▲ Malala Yousafzai survived an assassination attempt in 2012 aged 15 when she was shot by the Taliban in Pakistan for demanding the right of girls to have an education. She recovered after being treated in hospital in Birmingham and continues to campaign for girls' rights. She was jointly awarded the Nobel Peace Prize in 2014 with Kailash Satyanth, a 60-year-old Indian who has for 30 years been a leader of the global movement to end child slavery.

Case study

My name is Jonas. I come from Senegal in West Africa. Ours is a small country. Fortunately, there is no war here, so I am safe.

I would like to attend more time at school, but I can't. Every day, I have to get water for my mother to help feed the family. It's a 1.5 hour walk each way. I must do this twice per day. So I end up walking 6 hours a day, just to make sure we've got clean water. It's not so bad on the way there, but it's hard work on the way back, as the water is heavy.

There's no time for me to go to school. I know my education is suffering, but the water has to come first.

In pairs

Imagine you have to spend six hours a day just getting water. What things in your life would you have to give up?

For your file

Use the internet to research Plan International's `Because I am a girl' campaign. Write a short article explaining what it is and what it hopes to achieve.

Aim To examine how the news agenda is created and to explore the power of the media in shaping people's opinions

How powerful is the media?

With the development of the media, its power to shape our everyday lives has increased. Organisations such as the BBC – which controls many radio stations, a news channel, a website and bulletins on its other TV channels – can shape public opinion. Similarly, news groups such as Rupert Murdoch's News Corporation – which owns Sky News, *The Times* and *The Sun* newspapers, along with their corresponding websites – are able to shape the news agenda.

Strict rules govern the broadcast media to ensure it is politically neutral, but this is not the case for newspapers. On an average weekday, over half the adult population in the UK still read a national daily newspaper. The political party a newspaper supports in a General Election is therefore very important.

Gatekeepers – people who control the news

There are many news stories that could be included in newspapers, on TV or on the radio. A news outlet, such as a newspaper or TV station, has to decide which stories to cover. On a 'fast news day' (one with a lot of news in 24 hours) there won't be time to cover some stories. On a 'slow news day' stories that are less important are more likely to be published.

A news outlet has to decide how much coverage to give to a particular story. A politician's speech may receive a front-page story in one newspaper, only to receive a brief mention inside another. The amount of coverage a story gets is known as 'column inches' – literally the amount of space a story gets in a particular publication.

A news outlet also has to decide what angle or 'spin' to give a story. This can be a positive, negative, supporting, challenging or critical angle.

These decisions are crucial because they influence how people think about a news story. News outlets are deciding what people should know, how important a story is, and how it should be interpreted. This is known as acting as a 'gatekeeper'.

The growth in the number of media outlets means that some media power is being diluted. With more text message and email alerts, along with blogs and Twitter, other forms of media have to compete for our attention. The more media outlets there are, the less influence an individual outlet has.

However, media corporations who own large sections of the media, means that they may be able to influence, or even dictate the news agenda.

In groups

Which do you think has more influence on public opinion – newspapers or TV? Give reasons for your views.

The BBC is required to be neutral, but is sometimes accused of left-wing bias. Is such criticism fair? Is the BBC sometimes guilty of bias in the way that it reports the news?

In groups

Discuss the role of gatekeepers. Imagine you are on the editorial committee of your school's weekly newspaper. List the issues that have arisen during the week. Rank them in order of importance, and decide which will be your lead story and which other two stories you will refer to on your front page. Compare your decisions with those of other groups. Discuss what this tells you about setting the news agenda.

For your file

Study and compare three different newspapers' front pages for the same day. Do they all have the same lead story? Do they give different amounts of space to different stories? Do they report stories from the same viewpoint?

Spin doctors

Governments, corporations and pressure groups also employ people to manipulate and influence the media. These people are known as 'spin doctors'. The term comes from America where pitchers try to give a spin to a baseball. The job of a spin doctor is to try to get the media to report a story from a certain angle.

Supporters of spin doctors claim that they are necessary to get an organisation's message across successfully. They also believe that spin doctors are useful because they can give additional information about a news story. Critics of spin doctors say that they distort stories. This leads to a managed news agenda, where it is difficult to see what is really going on.

▲ Alastair Campbell worked as a spin doctor for the former UK Prime Minister, Tony Blair.

The British Broadcasting Corporation (BBC)

The BBC, which was started in 1922, is now responsible for providing the major TV channels, BBC1 and BBC2, and the news channel BBC24. It also provides radio stations such as Radio 1 (popular music) and Radio 4 (news and current affairs) and a network of local radio stations. The BBC World Service broadcasts information throughout the world.

The BBC is unique in that it is funded by the licence fee. Everyone who owns a TV, or a computer capable of receiving TV programmes, must have a TV licence. This costs around £140 per year. Supporters of the BBC argue that this means that non-profitable programmes, such as regional news, children's educational programmes and other local programming will be created.

However, critics of the BBC have argued that it is unfair that the BBC receives all of the licence fee, while its main competitors, such as ITV and Channel 4, do not receive any money from this source. Instead, they have to rely on advertising. As a result, in 2009, the Government announced plans to give a small share of the licence fee to the commercial TV companies in the future to help fund regional news services.

In groups

Do you think spin doctors are a good idea? Or do they get in the way of a free media? Give reasons for your views.

For your file

Imagine that your school runs a Strictly Student Dancing event with individual entries from local schools. One of your school's entrants, calling himself Footloose Frank, reaches the semi-finals, where he is eliminated, following some harsh criticism from the judges about his performance. Write two versions of the story, one with a positive spin saying how well he did to get to the semi-finals, the other with a negative spin suggesting he did better in the competition than he should have done.

In pairs

"We shouldn't prop up the BBC by paying a licence fee. The BBC should have to pay for itself like all its competitors."

"The BBC provides a unique broadcasting service. The licence fee provides excellent value for money."

"Why should part of the licence fee go to ITV and Channel 4? They should have to support themselves like any other commercial companies."

Discuss these statements. Say which you agree with and why.

A free media?

Aim To discuss freedom of speech in the media

The idea of freedom of speech is key to modern democracy. Article 19 of the Universal Declaration of Human Rights states that "Everyone has the right to freedom of expression and opinion". In other words, people should be allowed to contribute to a debate – to freely give and receive ideas. This means that the media, where possible, should have as much freedom as is reasonable.

In the USA, there is a completely free media. Anyone can publish or broadcast what they like. For example, if you want to set up a radio station and broadcast your views to the world, there is nothing to stop you from doing so.

In the UK, there are stricter controls. If you want to set up a radio station, you must get a licence from the government. In the USA, you have some radio stations that broadcast extremist views. In the UK, a radio station could be refused a licence if it was suspected of wanting to broadcast racist views.

Controlling the press by limiting information is known as 'censorship'. Some people argue that there ought to be total freedom of the media. Here, people would be able to broadcast anything they liked. Others argue that there should be limits on what people can say in the media.

By contrast, the Internet is much more difficult to police, due to its size and international nature. The UK government can order a racist website to be shut down if it is based in the UK. However, if it is based in a country where there is freedom of the media, then there is nothing the UK government can do.

Should the media ever be controlled?

During the Second World War, the UK government assumed control of the media and decided what stories could and could not be printed. This was done to boost morale in order to help win the war. The government was acting in what is called the 'national interest'. This is the main reason, or excuse, given when a government wants to withhold or release only part of the information that is available to them.

During the Second Gulf War, the UK government was able to influence the news agenda in several different ways. It decided on the timing of stories – when to release information, the amount of information it was going to release, and the angle or 'spin' the story was given.

In pairs

Do you think there should be tighter controls when it comes to information on the Internet? Why? Give reasons for your views.

In groups

Discuss the circumstances in which you think the government would be right, for reasons of national security, to control the information reported by the media.

The Internet in the world – a case of inequality?

In order to use the Internet, people have to have access to it. One problem is that certain groups of people may have their access limited. In the UK, older people who are less familiar with new technology may have trouble accessing the Internet.

Other groups include people who are poor or unemployed. These people may not be able to access the Internet regularly, missing out on the best jobs or cheapest deals. Additionally, they may not be able to afford high-speed broadband when they do access it, so their use of the Internet may be restricted. Therefore, there is a danger of an information underclass being created.

The global picture

In the UK nearly 90% of the population have Internet access and over 85% of the population in Germany and Japan. But worldwide the figure is only 30%, with some African countries such as Somalia and Sierra Leone having less than 2%. The lack of cable, broadband coverage or wireless Internet means that as technology improves in more developed countries like the UK, less developed countries like Senegal in Africa are left behind. In addition, 80% of the world's Internet sites are written in English, yet English is only understood by 25% of the world's population. This creates a huge language barrier.

Case study: China

China is a key player in the media industry, as the country hosts 1 in 4 of the world's population. There are over 620 million Internet users in China, second only to the USA. However, although many people have Internet access, it is tightly controlled by the Chinese government.

The Chinese government censors information in three ways:

1 The publishers of all web pages in China must have a licence from the Chinese government.
2 The Chinese government controls the points where people can access the Internet.
3 There are strict rules about what political and religious information can be published and accessed in China.

For example, many overseas sites, such as the BBC World Service, cannot be accessed on the Internet in China.

Internet companies that provide web pages in China, such as Google, have been criticised for co-operating with the Chinese government in carrying out this form of censorship. This is because they are providing an Internet service only available under the Chinese government's conditions. Supporters of the Internet in China say that it is better to have some information rather than none at all.

In the last few years, the Chinese government has begun to crack down on teenagers' use of the Internet. Ways of doing this have included claiming that the Internet can be a dangerous addiction. In extreme cases, Chinese teenagers have been sent to military style boot camps, to cure them of their addiction to the Internet.

In pairs

Suggest measures that the government and local councils could take in order to prevent an information underclass existing.

In groups

Imagine if you could only access Internet sites approved by the British government. How much of an impact would this have on you?

Organise a debate on the motion: "This house believes that there should be total freedom of speech and access to the Internet."

Privacy versus public interest

Aim To discuss the question of press intrusion, privacy and public interest and to explore the increased use of social media

Everyone has the right to privacy. But if a person in public life does something immoral or indefensible does the public have the right to know? In what circumstances does the public's interest override a person's right to privacy? If a person in public life has an affair is it in the public interest for the press to publish the story or is that an intrusion into that person's privacy? What if the press discovers that an MP who is calling for a reduction of the number of illegal immigrants is employing an illegal immigrant as his cleaner? Where does the right to privacy end and the right of the public to know begin?

From *Private Lives, Public Concerns* by Derek Stuart

▲ Milly Dowler, the murdered schoolgirl whose phone was hacked by journalists.

Phone hacking

There was a public outcry when it was revealed that the *News of the World* had been paying people to hack into the phones not only of celebrities, politicians and members of the royal family, but also of the murdered schoolgirl Milly Dowler, relatives of deceased British soldiers and victims of the July 7 London bombings. As a result, the *News of the World* was closed and a number of arrests and convictions were made, most notably of the *News of the World's* former managing editor Andy Coulson.

In groups

Study this list of methods that investigative journalists can use in order to obtain information. Which do you think are acceptable methods? Which are unacceptable and should be illegal?

- Hidden newspaper photographer
- Hidden video/television camera
- Hidden microphone
- Reporter impersonating someone else
- Intercepting post
- Recording phone calls where reporter identifies himself
- Recording phone calls where reporter pretends to be someone else
- Hacking into someone's phone
- Intercepting emails
- Interviewing family and friends
- Interviewing work colleagues
- Interviewing a person's children
- Doorstepping
- Searching though household/office rubbish for relevant documents
- Information leaked from anonymous sources

In groups

Discuss the questions Derek Stuart raises in the paragraph above.

In pairs

Discuss these situations and say whether you think they are an invasion of privacy.

1 A premier league footballer has been to a night club and is photographed leaving the club having had too much to drink.

2 A prominent politician tells a racist joke at a private party. Someone who was present leaks the story to a journalist.

3 A member of a boy band is killed in a car accident and a reporter is sent to his parents' home to interview friends and relatives.

4 A reporter sees a well-known actor leaving a hospital and finds out that he has been diagnosed with cancer. He tells his editor and they plan to run the story.

Social media

The development of social media sites such as Facebook and Twitter means that people can not only communicate instantly with friends and family, but can comment on the news and post their views on any subject. Activists have been quick to realise that they can use social media to spread political and ideological propaganda and to attack their opponents.

Campaign of Harassment Against US Airman

A member of the United States Air Force and his family were subjected to a campaign of harassment by ISIS supporters after he uploaded pictures of a bombing raid on an ISIS stronghold in Iraq.

The airman was sent threats and hateful messages online in a coordinated campaign by terrorist sympathisers to intimidate military members and their families. His teenage son also received threatening messages.

According to Fox News the ISIS supporters rallied round an Arabic Twitter account which orchestrated the 'flashmob-style' attacks.

Source: Mail Online, 8 October 2014

Dealing with trolls

However hurtful or untrue their comments, never respond. Ignore the trolls. Don't be drawn into a slanging match. Remember that trolling is not welcomed on most moderated sites. Bullying is a violation of Facebook policy and Twitter has rules about making threats. Report the trolls by clicking the Report Abuse button.

In groups

1 "Trolls abuse the right we all have to free speech. Trolls should be exposed and silenced." Do you agree?

2 What do you think is the best way to deal with Internet trolls?

In groups

"Social networking is meant to be social and social implies fun and friendly. But this is not always the case. Online bullying and victimisation is on the increase and with the web being free and people having the right to freedom of expression, hurtful comments and trolling cannot always be monitored or stopped. Should Facebook and other networks try and rein in this behaviour? Some would argue yes because of the impact it has on victims and their families, while others would say people have the right to say what they like, regardless of how hurtful and disgusting it is."

Source: wearesocialpeople.com

Discuss this view.

Sexism and sexual harassment

What is sexism?

Sexism is when we treat a person differently purely because they are of a particular sex. Imagine a man and a woman both applying for the same job. Both people have similar backgrounds and qualifications. An employer may want to employ the man because the office is full of men and he feels the man would fit in better. However, this is illegal, because it is sexual discrimination – treating someone differently because of his or her sex.

Why is sexism damaging?

Sexism is present in our society in many ways. An example of sexism towards women is that women are often paid less than men who do the same job, and are often given less responsibility. In the UK, employers are also often accused of allowing women to progress to a certain level within a company, but no further – this is known as the 'glass ceiling'.

Sexism is damaging because it doesn't allow people to fulfil their potential. In the case of sexism towards women, it can hold women back, deny them opportunities, and make it harder for them to assert their independence.

Aim To examine what sexism and sexual harassment are, and to explore how to challenge them

In groups

1 Look at the examples below of sexism that you may have encountered. What other examples can you think of?

"Girls are better at languages, but boys are better at science."

"Girls are brighter than boys."

"Boys are better than girls at sport."

"It's more important for a boy to have a career than a girl."

2 Make a list of attitudes that you think are sexist. Compare your lists in a class discussion.

In groups

Discuss the statements below. Which do you agree with? Give reasons for your views.

"Women are often judged by their appearance rather than their ability to do a job."

"Even today, there are still some jobs that most people regard as 'men's jobs' and other jobs that people regard as 'women's jobs'."

"Why it is that when a man is looking after the children at home people look down on him?"

"We need stronger laws when it comes to sexual discrimination. And women should stand up for themselves – whenever you find sexual discrimination, report it!"

Sexual harassment

Sexual harassment is another form of sexism. This is when a person repeatedly pesters or is a nuisance towards another person, through their behaviour. This behaviour could include making sexual advances. Although sometimes the behaviour may appear to be 'innocent', to the person on the receiving end it can be uncomfortable, off-putting, and even threatening.

Case study: street harassment

Shouting at girls, is, in fact, an act of hostility. No one shouts sexual remarks at someone he or she loves or respects. Men and boys who do shout at women do it because they think treating women as objects is 'cool', and that it gives them the upper hand.

Sometimes a man will harass a woman as an expression of his own insecurity – dislike for himself, perhaps, and an inability to believe that any female could really like him. Other times the hostility is based on race or class. Some workmen, for example, seem to enjoy harassing women dressed in office clothing. The hostility can be disguised as flattery, but often it's right out there in the open.

Source: *Stand up for Yourself* by Helen Benedict

In groups

1 Study the examples of behaviour below. Which do you think qualify as sexual harassment? Why?

- Wolf whistling
- Putting your arm around someone
- Saying somebody looks nice, once
- Asking somebody out once
- Refusing to take 'No' for an answer when someone doesn't want to go out with you
- Saying somebody looks nice, repeatedly.

2 Discuss what you have learned about street harassment. Why do you think some men shout sexual remarks at women?

3 Think about the situation of a group of women out drinking on a Friday night. Are there ever situations when women behave in a similar way to men?

For your file

Design a poster as part of a campaign against sexual harassment. Think about the key messages you would like to get across.

In groups

Sexism in the workplace can be quite common. Discuss what action you should take in each of the situations below.

- One of your work colleagues, a boy with long hair, is told by the boss to get it cut, because he 'looks like a girl'.

- A group of young men put a photo of a topless female model up in a staffroom and joke about it in front of the women who share the staffroom.

- You are a married woman, and during a job interview one of the interviewers asks you whether or not you have children, or are planning to have them.

Homosexuality and homophobia

Aim To understand what homosexuality and homophobia are, and the different attitudes towards homosexuality that exist

What is homosexuality?

Homosexuality is when a person is attracted to members of the same sex. Men who are attracted to other men are called 'gay'. Women who are attracted to women are known as 'lesbians'. Sometimes, a person's sexual orientation may involve attraction towards members of both sexes. These people are known as 'bisexuals'.

Many myths have grown up about homosexuals. Here are some of them:

▼ Homosexual couples are often discriminated against

MYTH: "You can tell homosexuals from their appearance and behaviour." ✗

REALITY: Not true. Some people think that all gay men are 'effeminate' and that all lesbians are 'butch'. The fact is that there is as much variety in the appearance and behaviour of homosexuals as there is among heterosexuals.

MYTH: "Homosexuals dislike people of the opposite sex." ✗

REALITY: Not true. Homosexuals may like and dislike people of either sex, just as heterosexuals do.

MYTH: "Homosexuals fancy everyone who is of the same sex as them." ✗

REALITY: Not true. Just because you like someone of one sex, doesn't mean you like everyone of that sex. It's the same for homosexuals.

How society discriminates against homosexuals

A fear of homosexuals is known as 'homophobia'. This can lead to prejudice and harassment – where people treat homosexuals badly purely because of their sexuality. In the UK such behaviour is against the law. For example, you can't turn down a person for a job just because of their sexual orientation.

'Hate crimes' are when people attack homosexuals purely because they are homosexual. However, hate crimes are not just directed at people who are homosexual. The law imposes heavier penalties in recognition of this type of crime.

There are also more subtle forms of discrimination that occur every day against homosexuals in the UK. Because most people are heterosexual, the rules that govern our society have advanced to promote heterosexuality and discriminate against homosexuality.

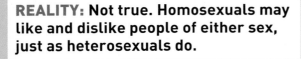
In pairs

1 Discuss the myths about homosexuality (above). Can you think of any other myths?

2 Why do you think these myths might be damaging?

In groups

Do you think homosexuals are discriminated against in the UK?

Different attitudes towards homosexuality

In the UK, there are different attitudes towards homosexuals and homosexuality. For instance, the Catholic Church disapproves of the act of two people of the same sex making love. Some Methodist Christians believe that a permanent relationship that includes love is an appropriate way of expressing sexuality, whatever the sexes of the two partners in the relationship.

Campaigning groups, such as Stonewall, believe that hatred of homosexuals is a social evil, equal to racism and sexism. Stonewall argues there should be equal treatment for all men and women, whatever their sexual orientation.

▲ A Stonewall demonstration

WHY IS HOMOPHOBIA DAMAGING?

Preconditioned by things such as TV and advertising, it's assumed that every boy and girl is straight (heterosexual)...

There is tremendous pressure on us all to conform, to become objects of desire to the opposite sex, to get married and to have children...

The problem is intensified by the fact that in our culture there still exists a taboo against homosexuality. This taboo exists mainly because there is an old idea that 'sex equals reproduction' and as loving someone of the same sex can't produce babies, many see it as 'unnatural', 'abnormal', or even 'perverted'.

Insulting words such as 'poofter', 'faggot', 'queer', 'bender' and 'dyke' have been invented to reinforce this prejudice and they cause a lot of harm. These prejudices make many homosexual people feel that if they are attracted to the same sex there must be something wrong with them and they end up feeling bad about themselves and their sexuality.

For your file

Someone you know is being bullied because she is a lesbian. Write about how you would deal with this situation if it happened (a) at school and (b) outside school.

Source: *Homosexuality* by Rosalyn Chissick

In pairs

Look at the statements below. Which do you agree with? Give reasons for your views.

"Homosexuals should be entitled to exactly the same rights as heterosexuals, and be treated in exactly the same way."

"I'm all for homosexual rights. But some gay people go out of their way to emphasise their sexuality. In order to be treated equally, they should act exactly like other people and not make a big thing of it."

In groups

Discuss the situations below and what you should do in each case to challenge homophobia.

One of your friends is getting bullied by a group of other teenagers, because they have discovered that he is gay.

You see someone spraying homophobic graffiti outside a flat where a lesbian couple live.

Stress

Aim To understand what stress is and what causes it, and to explore ways of dealing with stress

What is stress? Erica Stewart explains

Anxiety is a feeling of uneasiness or tension about what will happen in the future. It is something that everyone experiences, and it's quite normal to feel anxious from time to time.

The teenage years are years of change and it is only natural that you should feel apprehensive about some of the new situations that you have to face. As you grow up, you are expected to take more control of your own life and to make your own decisions. You have to start thinking about what career path you are going to take and cope with the pressures of preparing for important exams.

Your relationships with other members of your family change. You may develop a close relationship with a boyfriend or girlfriend and you have to learn how to handle the strong emotions that this involves. There may be pressures from other friends, too, for example to take risks you are unsure you want to take.

All these things can make you feel anxious. A certain amount of anxiety is good for you. If you didn't worry about doing something risky, you might do something you will later regret. If you didn't feel anxious about passing your exams, you might not bother to do enough revision.

But too much anxiety can make you ill. When you get over-anxious you are said to be suffering from 'stress'. Some teenagers get stressed because the everyday pressures of coping with life at home and/or at school get on top of them. Others may develop stress because of a life-changing event, such as the death of someone, parents separating or divorcing, or moving to a different area to live.

What stresses you out?

"I got stressed out when my parents were splitting up. The atmosphere in the house was terrible." Xavier

"I get really wound up about my schoolwork. I used to cope with it, but there seems so much of it now. I worry so much that I can't seem to get started." Dom

"My friends put pressure on me to do things I don't really want to do. I worry that they'll exclude me from the group if I don't join in." Taz

In groups

1 Discuss the different reasons these teenagers give for feeling stressed.

2 What other things can cause teenagers stress? Make a list of what you think are the top five causes of stress for teenagers.

3 Compare your lists in a class discussion. Discuss whether the causes of stress for boys are different from the causes of stress for girls.

Signs of stress

- Bad temper
- Feeling sick or having constant 'butterfly' nerves in your stomach
- Difficulty with sleeping or waking up early
- Difficulty with concentrating at school
- Frequent headaches
- Crying a lot
- Loss of appetite or increased appetite
- Biting your nails

Dealing with stress

If you think you are under stress, do two things straight away. Talk to somebody about your problems and put some time into each day to relax. You need to feel that you are in charge of your life. You may need to accept that there are some things you are not able to do. Sort out what's most important and make decisions.

People don't all deal with stress equally well. People who are generally confident and feel they can cope with life's problems will certainly manage better than people who feel helpless. So if you can convince yourself that the problem is not as great as it seems, you'll manage better. Positive thinking really does help.

Source: *Growing Up* by Merlion Publishing

Exercise can help with depression

Advice for beating the blues

- Get regular exercise. Physical exercise is good for thet mind as well as for the body. Studies show that if you exercise regularly, your body creates more beta endorphins (natural hormones that make you feel better about yourself). Also, if you are physically tired you will sleep well.

- Don't hold things in. Have a good cry if you can, and talk to anyone who'll listen sympathetically.

- Make a list of all the things you really enjoy in life and try to do some of them.

- Give yourself something to look forward to every day – like visiting a good friend, watching a favourite film, or buying a magazine.

Source: *Growing Up* by Merlion Publishing

In pairs

1 Study the two articles above on how to deal with stress. Draw two columns. In the first column, list each piece of advice about how to deal with stress. In the second column, list the reasons for the advice.

2 What do you think are the most important pieces of advice in the two articles?

For your file

You receive an email from a friend who has moved to another school. She's feeling stressed out. Draft a reply to her, suggesting some things she might do to try to relieve her stress.

Depression

Aim To explore what depression is and different types of depression, and to examine ways of coping with depression

In pairs

Study the two articles and write down 10 things you have learned about depression. Compare your lists in a group or class discussion.

What is depression?

Depression is one of the most common but also one of the most misunderstood medical conditions. It is estimated that one in four people will suffer from depression at some point in their lifetime.

People who suffer from depression usually experience persistent sadness with feelings of helplessness and hopelessness. These feelings may make it difficult to carry out normal daily activities.

Depression is a condition with a wide range of physical and psychological symptoms that sometimes make it hard to recognise and understand. Depression can affect anyone and does not reduce your value as a human being.

It is important to remember that:
- depression can affect anyone at any age.
- depression is not connected with, and does not develop into, insanity.
- depression can be treated.
- there is no need to cope alone.

Source: *The Young Person's Guide To Stress*, Depression Alliance

Types of depression

- **Reactive depression** – This is triggered by a traumatic, difficult or stressful event, and people affected will feel low, anxious, irritable, and even angry. Reactive depression can also follow a prolonged period of stress and can begin even after the stress is over.

- **Endogenous depression** – This is not always triggered by an upsetting or stressful event. Those affected by this common form of depression will experience physical symptoms such as weight change, tiredness, sleeping problems and low mood, as well as poor concentration and low self-esteem.

- **Bipolar disorder (manic depression)** – People with bipolar disorder experience mood swings, with 'highs' of excessive energy and elation, to 'lows' of utter despair and lethargy. Delusions or hallucinations can also occur. Most people with this condition have their first episode in their late teens or early twenties.

- **Seasonal Affective Disorder (SAD)** – This type of depression generally coincides with the winter months. It is linked to the shortening of daylight hours and a lack of sunlight. Symptoms will include wanting to sleep excessively and having cravings for carbohydrates or sweet foods. Special 'light boxes' can be used to treat this kind of depression.

- **Post-natal depression** – Many new mothers will experience 'baby blues', such as mood swings, crying spells and feelings of loneliness, three or four days after giving birth. Post-natal depression lasts for much longer and includes symptoms such as panic attacks, sleeping difficulties, having overwhelming fears about dying, and feelings of being unable to cope.

Source: *Everything You Need to Know About Depression*, Depression Alliance

Coping with depression

Erica Stewart offers advice on things you can do if you're depressed, which can help to lift your mood.

- Do something relaxing. Have a bath, play your favourite music, read a book or magazine.
- Get active. Exercise reduces stress, so go for a walk or a bicycle ride, do some dancing or kick a ball around in the park.
- Eat healthily. Your diet can affect your mood, so try to eat regular meals and make sure you get enough healthy foods such as fresh fruit and vegetables.
- Express your feelings. Write about them in a diary or journal, or write a song or a poem, or paint a picture. Putting your feelings into words or images can help you to understand them.
- Share your feelings. Talking to someone about how you feel can help you to understand more clearly what is making you depressed.

TALK TO SOMEONE

YoungMinds, the children's mental health charity, offers some advice.

Talking to someone might help you feel more able to cope. Try to talk to someone you like and trust. This might be one of the following:

- friend
- brother or sister
- grandparent
- parent or carer
- aunt or uncle
- friend's parent.

Other people you could talk to may include:

- teacher
- school counsellor
- social worker
- school nurse
- youth worker.

You can find out about places where young people can go for help: call Youth Access on 020 8772 9900 (Mon–Fri, 9am–5pm), or email: admin@youthaccess.org.uk

Ways to help a friend if they're unhappy or feeling depressed

- Listen and try to be sympathetic.
- Don't expect them to just snap out of it.
- Don't criticise or tease them.
- Try and get them to talk about how they feel.
- Be patient and allow them time to talk.
- Try to help them look for further help.

Source: *Do You Ever Feel Depressed?* by YoungMinds

In pairs

1 Discuss things you can do to help yourself if you are suffering from depression.

2 List the people you can talk to if you are depressed. Who do you think would be the best person to speak to?

3 Discuss how you can help a friend who is depressed. Make a list of what you would do.

For your file

Use the Internet to find out more about depression among teenagers and how to deal with it. Useful websites include: www.depressionalliance.org and www.youngminds.org.uk.

Sexually transmitted infections (STIs)

Aim To understand what sexually transmitted infections are and how to protect yourself against them

Be smart, be protected

More than 200 people a day are infected with chlamydia in the UK. Know the facts so you don't put yourself, or others, at risk...

If you're having sex you're at risk of catching an STI, caused by germs that can be passed on during sexual contact. Some STIs make you feel uncomfortable, others, like HIV (the virus that causes AIDS) can be life threatening. When used properly, condoms give a great deal of protection against most STIs, including HIV, chlamydia and gonorrhoea, but they are not a 100% guarantee against genital warts or herpes (or getting pregnant!).

1 latex condom
1 préservatif en latex
1 condón de látex

How can I avoid catching an STI?

- **Always use condoms for any type of sexual contact, including oral sex.**
- **Make sure the condom goes on before any contact between the penis and your body.**
- **Make sure you and your boyfriend know how to put a condom on.**
- **Say 'NO' to sex with any partner who doesn't want to use a condom – no excuses.**
- **Don't have sex until you're absolutely 100% sure that you want to.**

The most common STIs

Chlamydia
Symptoms include: creamy discharge from the penis or vagina; bleeding between sex; irregular periods; pain during sex or when urinating. 70% of girls and 50% of boys who have this disease show no symptoms at all. Untreated, it can lead to pelvic inflammatory disease and possibily infertility.

Genital warts
Symptoms include: itchy (not painful) lumps or bumps on the skin anywhere in the genital area.

Gonorrhoea
Symptoms include: yellow or green discharge from the penis, vagina or anus; bleeding and spotting after sex or between periods; pain when passing urine or during sex.

Genital herpes
Symptoms include: painful blisters on the skin anywhere in the genital area; swollen glands in the groin; fever; feeling unwell; pain passing urine or during sex.

Syphilis
Symptoms include: ulcers in the genital area or mouth; a rash may appear on the body and hands. If treated, it will heal in a few weeks. Untreated, syphilis can lead to problems with hearing, heart or nervous system.

In pairs

Write down what you have learned about STIs. How are they caught? How can you avoid catching them? How can you tell whether you have an STI?

Case study: Tim's story

Tim, 17, tells how he coped when he discovered he'd caught an STI

"Becky and I had been seeing each other for a month when we started sleeping together. At first we used condoms because I was worried about getting her pregnant, but when she said sex would be better without them she went on the Pill and we stopped using condoms.

Things were great until Becky's ex-boyfriend contacted her to say he was suffering from an STI – chlamydia – so she went for a test and discovered she had it too.

I knew she might have passed it on to me, so I went to see the doctor. She took a urine sample and I had to wait a week for the results.

When I went back, the doctor told me the test was positive. The doctor was great and said it was unlikely to cause any long-term damage. She prescribed antibiotics and the chlamydia cleared up.

Now I always use a condom. If someone tries to convince you to have sex without a condom, don't do it! Wearing a condom is a lot better than what I had to go through."

Source: J17

Before you do it, talk about it

Erica Stewart says: talk first, then decide whether or not to have sex

The questions you need to ask your partner are:

- **How many previous partners have you had?**
- **Did you ever have unsafe sex with any of them?**
- **Have you ever had an STI or been tested for one?**
- **What precautions are we going to take against catching an STI from one another?**
- **Do you intend to sleep with anyone else during our relationship?**

If you can't have such a discussion about your relationship, or do not trust your partner to answer truthfully, then you need to ask yourself: Does this person really care about me? Do I really want to have sex with a person who can't talk about such important things? Is it worth the risk?

What does safer sex involve?

Safer sex involves:

- Using contraception to prevent an unplanned pregnancy.
- Using protection to reduce the risk of catching an STI.
- Abstaining from sexual activities that might put you at serious risk of infection.
- Knowing your partner's sexual history before you have sex together, so that you can make an informed choice about whether or not to have sex with them.

In pairs

Discuss the statements below and say why you agree or disagree with them.

"Teenagers must learn to be selective about their sexual partners if they want to avoid catching an STI." **Health expert**

"It's ridiculous to suggest you should quiz your partner before you have sex. Do you really think they'll give honest answers?" **17-year-old girl**

"I don't intend to have sex before I'm married. It's common sense to wait – for health reasons as well as moral reasons." **18-year-old girl**

"What's the big deal? If I get an STI, I'll get it treated." **19-year-old boy**

In pairs

Discuss Tim's experience. Was she just unlucky, and what has she learned?

For your file

Imagine you have been asked by the Health Protection Agency to design a poster to warn young people about the risks of STIs. What messages do you want to put across?

HIV and AIDS

Aim To explore what the facts are about HIV and AIDS, and to examine attitudes to AIDS

HIV and AIDS: your questions answered

What are HIV and AIDS?

HIV stands for the Human Immunodeficiency Virus, which damages the immune system that protects the body from infection. It is sometimes called the AIDS virus, because it is the virus that can lead to the development of AIDS.

AIDS stands for Acquired Immune Deficiency Syndrome. People who have AIDS pick up infections more easily, because the body's protection system has been destroyed. These infections can cause death.

How can you get infected with HIV?

The HIV virus is present in an infected person's bodily fluids – their blood, and their semen or vaginal fluids. The main ways of transmission are:

- through unprotected sexual intercourse
- sharing needles or syringes if you are a drug user. Other possible ways of infection include:
- getting tattooed or pierced by equipment that hasn't been sterilised after being used on an infected person
- sharing a razor with an infected person.

In the past, some people were infected as a result of receiving blood transfusions of infected blood, but blood in many countries is now tested to make sure it doesn't carry the virus.

How can you protect yourself from getting infected?

At present, there is no vaccine that protects against HIV. The way to protect yourself is to practise safer sex.

- Always use a condom when having vaginal, anal or oral sex.
- Discuss your partner's previous sexual experiences with them before consenting to sex.
- Don't be pressurised into having unprotected sex.

Who is most at risk from HIV?

Anyone who practises unsafe sex. Most people who become infected do so as a result of sex between men and women. However in the developed world, certain groups are more at risk. These include:

- homosexual and bisexual men
- intravenous drug users
- people who have been sexually active in countries where HIV is widespread
- anyone who has sex with someone from these high-risk groups.

How can you tell if you're infected?

There are no immediate symptoms. The only way to find out if you have HIV is to have a blood test, but it takes three to six months for the virus to be detectable in the body. You can get advice about having a test from your local Genito-Urinary Medicine (GUM) clinic.

What happens if you become infected?

Most people who are HIV-positive will develop health problems, but it can take 10 or more years for AIDS to develop. However, even though people who are HIV-positive don't show any signs of illness, they are still infected and can pass it on to others.

Can AIDS be cured?

At present, there is no cure for AIDS, but there are drugs that you can take which can slow down the speed at which it develops.

Myths about HIV infection

You will NOT get HIV:

- by drinking from a glass or eating from a plate that has been used by a HIV-positive person.
- from hugging or shaking hands with someone who is HIV-positive.
- if someone sneezes; the virus doesn't travel through the air.
- if you're bitten by an infected insect, or if you donate blood at a blood transfusion unit.

Source: *Sex Ed* by Dr Miriam Stoppard

In pairs

Draw up a quiz consisting of statements about HIV and AIDS, some of which are 'True' and some of which are 'False'. Join up with another pair and answer each other's quiz.

Case study: Ellen's story

Ellen discovered she was HIV-positive when she was 16. She went for a test when she found out that her boyfriend's previous girlfriend was a drug user and had developed AIDS.

"I didn't expect the test to be positive," she remembers. "When it was, it felt like being given a death sentence. For months, I was just numb, I couldn't take it in."

Now, three years on, she is at college and enjoying life. She has recently started taking a combination of drugs to keep the HIV under control. "I'm on 24 pills a day, and they've all got to be taken at the right times. It's hard to get used to, and sometimes they make me feel really sick. But I know they're my best hope. I try not to think about the future too much; I just concentrate on today and try to get as much out of life as I can."

Source: *Sexually Transmitted Diseases* by Jo Whelan

In pairs

What is your attitude to HIV and AIDS? Read the statements below. Decide which of the views you most agree with. Share your thoughts in a class discussion.

> "AIDS concerns me, so I'm going to make sure I always have sex using a condom and avoid high-risk activities."

> "I'm worried sick about catching the HIV virus. I'd rather not have sex than take the risk of catching it and developing AIDS."

> "AIDS is like any other disease you might catch. Life's a lottery. The thought I might get AIDS isn't going to stop me from having sex with whoever I fancy."

People with HIV living longer

Cocktails of HIV drugs are helping patients live longer

The medication used to treat HIV is known as combination anti-retroviral therapy (Cart).

Advances in treatment have 'transformed HIV from being a fatal disease into a long-term chronic condition,' a University of Bristol study said.

It found that an HIV-positive person starting Cart treatment at the age of 20 will on average live another 43 years to 63.

Source: Sky News

In pairs

1 What do you learn from Ellen's story about what life is like for someone who is HIV-positive?

2 What is the difference between a fatal disease and a chronic medical condition? Why is HIV now described as a chronic condition?

In groups

Imagine you are part of a government team with the task of organising a campaign to educate young people about the dangers of unsafe sex. How would you get your message across? Discuss ideas for a campaign and draw up a proposal to share with the rest of the class.

Drugs: the risks

Aim To explore the reasons why young people take drugs, to examine the risks, and to provide information about ecstasy

Why do young people take drugs?

"I started smoking spliffs when I met my boyfriend Jason. He's three years older than me and he was really into it. I thought I'd look young if I didn't join in." Natasha, aged 15

"Taking drugs helps me to relax and I enjoy the buzz they give me." Neil, aged 17

"I take speed when I go out 'cos it gives me more energy and I find it easier to chat up girls. It makes me more confident. It's pretty rank the next day though – I feel really tired and depressed." Matt, aged 18

Let's face it – drugs are a fact of life. At some stage you or one of your mates are going to be offered something. Yeah, loads of drugs are illegal and you're not meant to take them – but at the end of the day the only person who can make those decisions about your lifestyle is you.

The important thing is that when you make those choices you know what you're doing and what's involved.

Source: *Tell It Like It Is* by Katie Masters

So what's the deal?

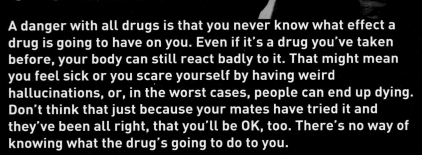

A danger with all drugs is that you never know what effect a drug is going to have on you. Even if it's a drug you've taken before, your body can still react badly to it. That might mean you feel sick or you scare yourself by having weird hallucinations, or, in the worst cases, people can end up dying. Don't think that just because your mates have tried it and they've been all right, that you'll be OK, too. There's no way of knowing what the drug's going to do to you.

Another danger is that when you're given a drug, you don't really know what's in it. Some dealers try and make a profit by adding cheaper ingredients into the drug. So they'll tell you they're selling ecstasy – and what you get is ecstasy mixed up with something else.

Finally, there are the dangers involved in getting the drugs into your body. Injecting drugs is the most dangerous way of taking them. If people share their injecting equipment, they run the risk of contracting blood diseases like HIV or hepatitis. Also, the user doesn't know how much of the drug is going in and that means they're more likely to overdose. If they miss the vein when they inject, they can end up with abscesses and gangrene.

In pairs

What are the reasons why young people take drugs? Make a list and put the reasons in order of importance, starting with what you think is the main reason. Compare your views in a group discussion.

In pairs

1 What do you consider to be the main risks involved in drug taking?

2 Discuss how young people obtain drugs. What is your attitude towards people who sell drugs to young people?

Source: *Tell It Like It Is* by Katie Masters

Ecstasy FACTFILE

- Taking ecstasy (or Es) is a gamble. Many tablets are not pure ecstasy. Because you never know what's in a tablet, you may get a negative reaction to whatever the ingredients are.

- It can take an ecstasy tablet between 20 minutes and an hour to kick in. Some people have taken another tablet thinking the first one hasn't worked and have given themselves a double dose.

- You don't know how ecstasy will affect you personally. The drug seems to make people both calm and energetic, but it can cause anxiety, panic attacks and confusion.

- Ecstasy affects your body's temperature control. If you dance for long periods without stopping regularly to chill out, you run the risk of overheating and dehydration. Users are advised to sip water or a non-alcoholic drink every hour. However, drinking too large a quantity of fluids after taking ecstasy can be very dangerous, so no more than a pint is recommended.

- The comedown from taking ecstasy (the 'ecstasy blues') can leave you feeling tired and depressed.

- No one is sure what the long-term effects are. There is some evidence that ecstasy use may cause brain damage with sustained memory loss and an increased risk of depression. Use of ecstasy has also been linked to liver and kidney problems.

▲ Clubbers taking ecstasy can run the risk of dehydration

Legal highs

A danger with all drugs is that you never know what effect a drug is going to have on you. Take the case of so-called legal highs like Pandora's Box, a cannabis-like drug which can be bought online. It's legal. But is it safe? Using it can cause paranoia, anxiety, breathing problems, heart palpitations, sweating, vomiting and collapse.

The problem with so-called 'legal highs' is you never know what it is you are taking. The packaging may describe what the ingredients are, but you can't be sure that's what they actually contain.

Legal highs cannot be sold for human consumption. So suppliers get round the law by saying that they are research chemicals, incense, bath salts or plant food. If you are found in possession of a legal high and the police aren't sure what the substance is, they can take it from you and detain you while it is analysed.

In groups

1 Discuss why you think people take ecstasy. What do you consider to be the main risk?

2 How would you try to persuade a friend that taking a legal high is not worth the risk?

For your file

"What are the risks from taking ecstasy?" Treena

Use the information on this page to draft a reply to Treena.

Drugs and the law

Aim To discuss the drugs laws and to debate whether they should be changed

Drugs laws:
time for a change?

Drugs laws were introduced to protect people from harming themselves by taking substances that:

- are dangerous to their health
- might alter their behaviour by making them do odd things
- they might become addicted to.

The Misuse of Drugs Act 1971 prohibits the non-medical use of certain drugs. Drugs are classified according to how dangerous they are considered to be.

- Class A drugs include heroin, cocaine, ecstasy, LSD and magic mushrooms.
- Class B drugs include cannabis and speed.
- Class C drugs include ketamine.

It is illegal to possess, supply or manufacture these drugs, and punishments range from up to two years and a fine for possession of Class C drugs, to a maximum penalty of life imprisonment and a fine for supplying Class A drugs.

Some people argue that the drugs laws are unnecessarily harsh and old fashioned and should be repealed. They advocate legalising all drugs on the grounds that individuals should have the right to decide for themselves whether or not to take substances that might damage their health or endanger their lives, provided that they do not harm or endanger the lives of other people.

What happens if you decriminalise drugs?

In 2000 Portugal was spending huge amounts of money sending drug users to prison and on health care for people who were HIV positive from sharing needles.

So in 2001 Portugal took the controversial action of removing all criminal penalties for drugs use. Instead of being arrested for drug use, drug takers are sent to a Commission for the Dissuasion of Drug Addiction, a panel consisting of a psychologist, a social worker and a legal adviser.

The panel can refer the user for treatment at a rehabilitation centre and can fine someone who turns up in front of it again within six months. But it cannot send the person to prison.

There was concern that the policy would lead to an increase in drug use. But in fact it has led to a decrease, especially in the number of teenagers using drugs, and to a drop in HIV infections from using dirty needles. What has increased is the number of people seeking treatment for addiction, which has doubled.

The success of Portugal's policy has led Spain and Italy to introduce similar policies.

In groups

Prepare for a class debate on the motion: "This house believes that decriminalising drugs use would do more harm than good."

In pairs

1 Discuss why you think there are drugs laws.

2 Discuss what happened in Portugal when drug use was decriminalised. Do you think drug use in the UK should be decriminalised?

The terrible truth about cannabis

A definitive 20-year study into the effects of long-term cannabis use has demolished the argument that the drug is safe.

Cannabis is highly addictive, causes mental health problems and opens the door to hard drugs, the study found.

The study by Professor Wayne Hall, a drugs adviser to the World Health Organisation, found that:

- One in six teenagers who regularly smoke the drug becomes dependent on it.
- Cannabis doubles the risk of developing psychotic disorders, including schizophrenia.
- Cannabis users do worse at school. Heavy use in adolescence appears to impair intellectual development.
- One in ten adults who regularly smoke the drug become dependent on it and those who use it are more likely to go on to harder drugs.
- Driving after smoking cannabis doubles the risk of a car crash, a risk which increases substantially if the driver has had a drink.
- Smoking cannabis while pregnant reduces the baby's birth weight.

"If cannabis is not addictive," said Professor Hall, "then neither is heroin or alcohol. It is often harder to get people who are dependent on cannabis through withdrawal symptoms than for heroin."

The study found that those who try to stop taking cannabis often suffer anxiety, insomnia, appetite disturbance and depression. Even after treatment less than half can stay off the drug for six months.

Source: *The Daily Mail, 7 October 2014*

In groups

Discuss these views.

"Smoking cannabis isn't worth the risk."

"People like Professor Hall are scaremongers. Reports like this won't stop me using cannabis."

"The facts are clear, cannabis should be reclassified as a Class A drug."

"Cannabis is like alcohol. It's up to the individual to decide whether or not to use it. To try to ban it wouldn't work."

For your file

Imagine you are a member of a government think tank on drugs. What changes, if any, would you suggest making to the drugs laws? Give reasons for your views.

First aid: coping with an emergency

Aim To understand how to deal with an emergency and how to treat a casualty who is unconscious

Coping with a crisis

Ever wondered how you would cope in a crisis, for example, if a friend was attacked or wounded?

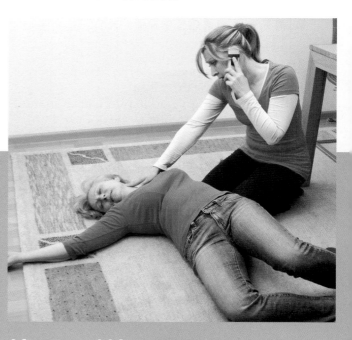

The basics Your personal safety must come first. Is the situation dangerous? Is the attacker still around? If in doubt, stay away and call the emergency services.

Punched or kicked If someone has been punched, kicked or hit with a blunt instrument, but not knocked unconscious, you may still need to call an ambulance. This is because blows to the head can cause concussion or bleeding into the brain, and blows to the abdomen can cause internal bleeding, both of which may be life threatening.

Someone who's been glassed The main danger here is fragments of glass that may still be in the wound. Don't pull fragments out of the wound, they cut on the way out as well as on the way in and may open up an artery. To stop the bleeding, avoid pressing down directly on the wound. Instead, press alongside the wound.

Beaten unconscious If someone has been knocked out but has regained consciousness, try to make them lie down and rest until medical help arrives. They may have hidden injuries that they are not aware of.

After a stabbing In the unlikely event that a knife remains in the wound, leave it there to help prevent further bleeding. Otherwise, apply pressure and lift up the affected part of the body. If there is a sucking noise and bubbling of blood from a chest wound, air is getting into the chest, which is very serious. Sit the person up and press firmly over the wound to stop any more air getting in, or if possible place a handkerchief or pad over the wound and tie it to them with a scarf.

When emergency services arrive Tell the ambulance crew what you saw and what's been done to the person, then let them take over.

Source: 'Emergency First Aid', www.thesite.org

The ABC of emergency first aid

When giving emergency first aid to an unconscious person, your priorities must always be ABC.

A ...is for Airway. Check that the passage between the mouth, nose, throat and windpipe is clear.

B ...is for Breathing. Check that the person is still breathing.

C ...is for Circulation. Check that the heart is still beating, and that the blood is still being circulated, by feeling for a pulse in the side of the neck.

If there are other people around, send someone for help or dial 999 yourself.

Dealing with unconsciousness

Knowing what to do in an emergency can save lives. Many deaths from road accidents occur from the person choking to death while lying unconscious. It is thought that many lives could have been saved if someone had just put the injured person in the recovery position (see below).

Unconsciousness can be caused by anything that interrupts the normal working of the brain. The most common causes of unconsciousness are heart attack, stroke, epilepsy, drug overdose, alcohol, head injury, diabetes, and poisoning.

Whatever has caused the patient to become unconscious may also have caused additional injuries. His breathing may have stopped, for example, or he may be bleeding severely. Your first priority is to deal with any of these life-threatening injuries.

Once this has been done, you can take steps to prevent the main threat to the unconscious patient: choking to death. He could choke on his own vomit or his tongue could obstruct his airway so that he cannot breathe. Putting the patient into the recovery position will make these things less likely.

You should NOT move any unconscious person who has had a bad fall or serious injury that may have damaged his spine. Leave him where he is until help arrives.

The recovery position

1 Place arm nearest you at a right angle.

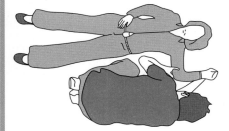

2 Move the other arm, as shown, with the back of their hand against their cheek. Then get hold of the knee furthest from you and pull up until foot is flat on the floor.

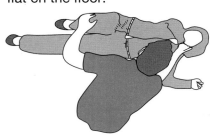

3 Pull the knee towards you, keeping the person's hand pressed against their cheek, and position the leg at a right angle.

4 Make sure that the airway remains open by tilting the head back and lifting the chin. Check breathing.

5 Monitor the casualty's condition until help arrives.

In groups

Draw up a list of Dos and Don'ts about giving first aid in a crisis. Discuss the reasons for each piece of advice.

In pairs

1 Explain what your priorities are when treating an unconscious person.

2 Discuss why an unconscious person is in danger of choking and what to do to prevent this from happening.

3 Practise putting each other in the recovery position.

Source: www.redcross.org.uk

Shock and resuscitation

Aim To examine how to treat someone for shock, and to know how to give artificial respiration to someone who has stopped breathing

What is shock?

Shock is the term used to describe the symptoms that happen when the organs of the body – especially the brain – are deprived of blood.

What we usually think of as shock – the feeling of faintness or shakiness that can follow a slight injury or an emotional upset – is caused by a temporary loss of blood to the brain. It is not life-threatening.

True medical shock occurs when there is actually less blood or body fluid available. When this happens, the body tries to keep up the blood supply to the brain at the expense of all other less important parts of the body.

What are the signs of shock?

After a severe accident, always watch for the following signs that indicate shock:

- Cold, clammy skin with heavy sweating
- Faintness, giddiness or blurring of vision
- Nausea or vomiting
- Thirst
- Confusion and anxiety
- Rapid, shallow breathing
- Rapid, feeble pulse.

Six steps to treat shock

1 Treat any obvious injuries.

2 Lay the person down on a blanket or rug to keep them warm. Reassure them.

3 Raise and support their legs above the level of their heart.

4 Loosen any tight clothing.

5 Call an ambulance.

6 Do not give them anything to eat or drink because they may later need a general anaesthetic in hospital.

Source: www.redcross.org.uk

For your file

Write an information sheet on shock. Include what shock is, what causes it, what the symptoms are, and how to treat it.

Mouth-to-mouth resuscitation

It is possible to save the life of a person who has stopped breathing by giving them mouth-to-mouth resuscitation. This provides the patient with artificial ventilation, but you need to be trained to do this properly.

It is important to act quickly because a person who has stopped breathing is not getting any oxygen. If their brain is deprived of oxygen for more than a few minutes, they will probably suffer permanent brain damage. They need an emergency supply to their lungs to help them to start breathing again for themselves.

This is how a first aider is trained to give mouth-to-mouth resuscitation:

1 Lie the person on their back, tilt their head back and gently pull their lower jaw forward. Sometimes this is sufficient to start them breathing again, by bringing the tongue forward away from the airway.

2 Put a finger into their mouth to make sure that nothing (e.g. sand, seaweed or vomit) is blocking the airway.

3 Hold the mouth open and pinch the nostrils together to stop the air breathed in from coming out through the nose. If possible, use a protective device over the mouth, such as a plastic bag with a hole in it, as this is more hygienic.

4 Take a deep breath, put your mouth over their mouth and blow into their lungs. Watch to make sure that their chest rises as the air enters their lungs, then falls when you take your mouth away. If it doesn't, then something is blocking the airway and you need to repeat stage 2.

5 Keep on breathing into the person's lungs until they start to breathe again for themselves or until medical help arrives. It may take some time for them to start breathing again, so do not give up if they don't start breathing straight away.

6 Once they start breathing again, put them in the recovery position (see page 63).

Cardio-pulmonary resuscitation (CPR)

If a casualty's heart has stopped beating, it may be possible to save their life by giving them chest compressions to keep their circulation going. These must be combined with artificial ventilation (see mouth-to-mouth resuscitation on the left). This combined process is known as cardio-pulmonary resuscitation, or CPR. It is essential to be trained in the use of this technique before you attempt it.

The sooner you start giving resuscitation, the more likely it is to be successful. It is also essential to call an ambulance as quickly as possible. Emergency ambulances carry a machine, called a defibrillator, which can start a person's heart beating again by applying a controlled electric shock. Paramedics can help to stabilise a casualty's condition until the person reaches hospital and receives further treatment and care.

For your file

Write an information sheet on each of the following:

- artificial ventilation – what it is, how it can save lives, and how to give it.
- CPR – what it stands for, and how chest compressions can keep a person alive until they receive expert medical attention.
- the importance of summoning an ambulance when someone needs resuscitation, and what a defibrillator is.

The European Union

Aim To understand what the European Union is and how it is organised

What is the EU?

EU stands for European Union. It is an international body made up of 28 different countries. The main aims of the EU are:

- To raise the quality of life for its citizens, through social development.

- To improve the economic position of its citizens, companies and countries by economic co-operation and development through economic growth.

- To promote common foreign and security policies and to create a secure environment for its citizens.

In just half a century of existence, the EU has delivered peace between its members and prosperity for its citizens. It has created a single European currency (the euro) and a borders-free 'single market' where goods, people and money move around freely. Membership has grown from six to 28 countries and the EU has become a major trading power.

The EU's success owes a lot to its unique nature and the way it works. It is not a group of states joined together in one country like the United States and it is not simply an organisation for co-operation between governments, like the United Nations (see page 74). The countries (member states) that make up the EU remain independent nations, but they pool their power in order to gain a strength and world influence none of them could have on their own.

How does the EU affect us?

The EU affects our daily lives in many different ways:

- The majority of UK trade is done with other member states, so the goods we buy in our shops often come from the EU.

- Our passports are EU passports. We have the freedom to travel and to live and work in any of the 28 countries of the EU.

- Many areas of our lives are covered by European law, in particular business, agriculture, the environment, discrimination and civil liberties.

In groups

1 Discuss the aims of the EU and what it has achieved during its existence.

2 What is unique about the EU's organisation? How is it different from the United States and the United Nations?

In pairs

List all the ways in which you think the EU affects you. Share your ideas in a class discussion.

For your file

Research the development of the EU from the formation of the European Economic Community at the Treaty of Rome in 1957 until the present. Draw a timeline marking in the key events and dates.

The main institutions of the EU

The European Council

- The European Council is a meeting of the heads of state and government of all the EU countries, plus the President of the European Union.
- It meets four times a year to agree overall EU policy and to review progress. It is the highest-level policy-making body in the EU, which is why its meetings are often called 'summits'.

The European Commission

- Its job is to propose new regulations or rules for the EU and to make sure that EU laws are implemented.
- Since 2004, there has been one Commissioner nominated from each member country. Commissioners are meant to leave behind loyalties to their countries and act for the good of the EU. They oversee the administration of the EU, and make sure that EU regulations are enforced.

The Council of the European Union

- This is the main legislative and decision-making body of the EU. It consists of one minister from each member state and meets nearly 100 times a year.
- It discusses proposals put forward by the European Commission. Different ministers meet according to each different area of policy. For instance, the 27 finance ministers, including the UK Chancellor of the Exchequer, will meet to discuss the EU budget, and the 28 foreign ministers will meet to discuss foreign affairs.

The European Parliament

- It is made up of representatives from member countries, known as Members of the European Parliament, or MEPs. The UK elects 73 MEPs by proportional representation.
- Its job is to scrutinise and develop policies within the EU. It discusses proposals made by the European Commission and can amend them, but its decisions are not binding. Although it is the only directly elected body, it is the least powerful of the main institutions of the EU.

European elections

Elections to the European Parliament are held once every five years, but there is considerable apathy among voters and turnout is much lower than for national elections. In the 2014 European elections in the UK the turnout was 35% compared to 66% in the 2010 general election.

▲ European Union summit at the EU Headquarters in Brussels on August 30, 2014

In groups

Discuss each of the main institutions of the EU. Who are its members? What is its function?

In groups

1 Why do you think turnout for European elections is lower than for national elections?

2 Imagine your group has been asked to plan a campaign to get more people to vote in European elections. What messages would you aim to put across? What would be the main features of your campaign?

For your file

Write an email to someone who is undecided about whether to vote in the European elections to persuade them that they ought to do so.

The UK and the EU

Aim To explore Britain's relationship with the EU

Britain and Europe

British people's attitudes towards Europe vary. Some are strongly in favour of the UK's membership of the EU. Many are less enthusiastic.

WHY BRITAIN SHOULD STAY IN THE EU

Should Britain quit the EU? My view is... it would be a historic error to pull out. Our economy would suffer if we quit. Our global influence would be diminished.

The UK now accounts for less than 1% of the world's population and less than 3% of global income. Each year that goes by, these numbers shrink a little. We will find it increasingly hard to get our voice heard on topics that affect our prosperity and well-being if we go it alone.

There is also a lot that is good with the EU. First and foremost is the single-market which gives British business access to the entire EU with its 500 million consumers. Free trade is one of the most powerful ways of boosting wealth. We would be foolish to compromise our access to this market.

Contrary to popular belief, EU membership doesn't cost us much, either. Our annual budget contribution, after taking account of money transferred back to the UK, is £8.3 billion. That's around half a per cent of our GDP, or £130 per person.

Source: Hugh Dixon in *The Independent*, 25 March 2014

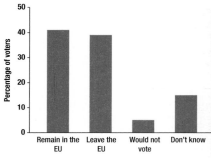

▲ In 2014 a You Gov poll asked people how they would vote in a referendum on Britain's membership of the EU.

Why the EU is good for Britain

■ **Free trade** Almost 50% of our exports go to the EU, which has free trade between its member states. This is good for UK businesses, which don't have to worry about quotas or import taxes.

■ **Investment in Britain** Foreign investors have put millions of pounds into the UK, because Britain is a member of the EU and is, therefore, a bridge to the single market.

■ **EU Structural Funds** Structural Funds are the large amount of money that is distributed among the most deprived areas of the EU. For many years they have contributed to investment and infrastructure across the UK, especially in Northern Ireland, Yorkshire and Cornwall.

■ **Influence in Europe** While we are in the EU we can be involved in EU decision-making. If Britain is outside the EU, we won't have a voice when European countries are making decisions that affect us.

■ **Influence outside Europe** Alone, Britain's influence in the world would be greatly reduced. Within the EU Britain would remain a leading partner in the biggest combined economy in the world.

In groups

Are you convinced by the arguments that Britain is better in the EU than out of it? How would you vote in a referendum on Britain's membership of the EU? Give your reasons.

The Treaty of Lisbon 2007

The Treaty of Lisbon introduced significant changes to the way the EU operates. It aimed to reform the EU's institutions to make them function better. However, opponents saw it as bringing the idea of a federal Europe closer, and as a threat to national sovereignty.

The changes included:

- the creation of an EU president who will serve a two-and-a-half-year term (replacing the system whereby countries took it in turns to hold the presidency of the European Union for six months)
- the creation of a more powerful foreign policy chief in order to give the EU a stronger voice in world affairs
- reform of the European Commission, reducing the number of commissioners from 27 to 18
- removal of the national veto, which allows member states to block legislation, in certain areas.

 **In groups**

Discuss the issue of the national veto. Do you think all decisions in the Council of the European Union should be made by a majority, or are there some policy areas e.g. taxation where the national veto should be retained?

The UK Independence Party

The UK Independence Party (UKIP) campaigns for Britain to withdraw from Europe.

UKIP argues that:

- Britain has lost the freedom to make its own decisions as EU regulations are decided in Brussels rather than by Parliament.
- The EU is centralized, bureaucratic and unaccountable,
- British taxpayers' money should be spent on British taxpayers, not used to subsidise 'fraud and corruption' in Brussels.
- Membership of the EU takes jobs away from British people, as workers from other countries are hired instead of British workers.
- Britain needs to retake control of its own borders, and the only people who should decide who can come into the UK to live and work are the British people themselves.
- Britain is an international trading nation. Instead of focusing on trade with the EU, we should be developing our trade with the rest of the world.

▲ A UKIP campaign billboard

 **In pairs**

Discuss the views below. Which do you agree with and why?

"We should withdraw from Europe completely."

"Europe should become one country and the UK should just be part of that country."

For your file

Are you a pro-European in favour of the further development of the EU or are you a Euro-sceptic? Would you ever consider voting for a UKIP candidate? Write a statement expressing your views and the reasons for them.

Aim To understand what NATO is and its political and military aims

What does NATO do?

NATO is the North Atlantic Treaty Organisation, of which the UK is a member. It was set up by 12 member states in 1949. Today it has 28 members. Twenty-five members are European countries, two of them – the USA and Canada – are North American, and one – Turkey – is Eurasian.

The aim of NATO is to protect the freedom and security of its members by military and political means.

▲ The NATO flag. The blue background represents the Atlantic Ocean. The circle stands for unity among member states. The compass rose symbolises the direction to the path of peace, which the member states strive for.

- **Political** – NATO promotes democratic values and encourages consultation and co-operation on defence and security issues to build trust and, in the long run, prevent conflict.

- **Military** – NATO is committed to the peaceful resolution of disputes. If diplomatic efforts fail, it has the capacity needed to undertake military operations. These are carried out under Article 5 of the North Atlantic Treaty of 1949 or under a UN mandate, alone or in co-operation with other countries and international organisations.

Article 5 of the North Atlantic Treaty states that an armed attack against a member state shall be considered an attack against them all, and if such an attack occurs they will take action including, if necessary, the use of armed force to restore and maintain the security of the North Atlantic area.

Ukraine and NATO

Any European state can apply to join NATO. Ukraine is not at present a member. However, a petition signed by 2 million Ukrainians has called for a referendum on whether Ukraine should apply for membership. Since Russia's annexation of the Crimea in 2014, support among Ukrainians for Ukraine to join NATO has grown. However, Russia strongly opposes Ukraine joining NATO.

Protecting the Baltic States

In 2014, as a result of Russia's annexation of Crimea and support for the rebels in the eastern Ukraine, NATO deployed several hundred US troops in Poland, Latvia, Lithuania and Estonia. The move was justified as giving confidence to these NATO members that NATO would take action to protect these states if necessary.

Originally it was intended that the troops would stay only until the end of 2014, but towards the end of 2014 it was decided that they should stay throughout 2015.

'There are going to be US Army forces here in Lithuania, as well as Estonia, Latvia and Poland for as long as is required to deter Russian aggression and to assure our allies,' stated the Commanding General of the US Army in Europe, Lieutenant-General Frederick Ben Hodges.

NATO in action

In September 2001 NATO invoked Article 5 after the terrorist attack on the World Trade Centre. It declared the attacks to be an attack against all 28 member countries and subsequently assisted the USA in its campaign against terrorism.

BOSNIA 1992–5

Following the Srebrenica massacre, NATO carried out air strikes against the Bosnian Serbs. These helped to bring an end to the conflict. NATO also provided the troops for the peacekeeping force which was deployed in the region at the end of the war.

AFGHANISTAN 2003–14

NATO led the International Security Assistance Force (ISAF) for which the UK supplied troops. ISAF aimed to establish security across the country, to enable Afghanistan to have a representative government and to ensure that it would never again be a safe haven for terrorists. NATO troops ceased to have a combatant role in Afghanistan at the end of 2014, but have stayed on in the country to support and advise Afghanistan's own army.

LIBYA 2011

NATO provided support for the Libyan people as they fought for freedom from the repressive rule of Colonel Gaddafi. NATO helped to enforce the embargo on the supply of arms to Libya and NATO planes, including British aircraft, flew 26,500 sorties to enforce a no-fly zone.

SYRIA 2014

NATO provided humanitarian aid to refugees who poured into neighbouring countries fleeing from the civil war.

▲ Three NATO fighter jets flying over Cardiff Bay during the 2014 summit meeting

▲ World leaders at the NATO summit in Cardiff, September 2014

▼ Dutch troops in Afghanistan soon to receive the NATO medal

In groups

Discuss the role that NATO has played in world affairs in the last 25 years. How important is it to Britain to be a member of NATO? What obligations and responsibilities does membership of NATO bring?

The UK and the Commonwealth

Aim To explore the UK's relationship with the Commonwealth, and how the Commonwealth works

What is the Commonwealth?

The Commonwealth of Nations (or the Commonwealth) is an international organisation made up of countries that were once part of the British Empire. It contains 53 member states, including over 2 billion people, making up almost one-third of the world's population.

▲ Prince Charles with the Commonwealth heads of government

The founder member of the Commonwealth was the UK. Other major countries within the Commonwealth include Canada, Australia, New Zealand, India, and Pakistan. Many African and Caribbean countries, as well as some islands in the Pacific, are also members.

The aims of the Commonwealth

The aims of the Commonwealth are similar to those of the EU (see pages 66–69) and the UN (see pages 74–75). Seven main aims promote the following:

1 International peace and order
2 Democracy
3 The rule of law
4 Good governance
5 Freedom of expression and human rights
6 Economic development
7 Social development

How the Commonwealth works

The Commonwealth meets formally once every two years in a member country. The 2015 meeting is in Malta. The British monarch, currently Queen Elizabeth II, is the Head of the Commonwealth and chairs these meetings.

The administrative headquarters of the Commonwealth are in London. The Commonwealth works to achieve its aims and to help countries in several different ways:

- By sending observers to check that elections are carried out properly, without fraud and intimidation.
- By providing training programmes for governments and companies within member countries, e.g. lawyers are sent to a less developed country to produce a report on how its legal system works.
- By sending advisers from one country to another to provide expertise and advice on economic development. For example, a group of irrigation experts are sent to an African country to train people on how to make the best use of their water supply.
- By holding conferences to discuss issues of importance to member countries. e.g. a conference is held on conflict prevention to encourage neighbouring governments to sort out their differences peacefully when they occur.

In groups

1 Discuss the different aims of the Commonwealth. Which do you think are the most important? Give reasons for your views.

2 Draw a spider diagram showing the different aims of the Commonwealth.

The aims of the Commonwealth

The member states of the Commonwealth share common goals – to strengthen democracy, to assist development and to preserve peace. The graphic shows the areas in which it promotes collective action.

If a country goes directly against the aims of the Commonwealth, it can be suspended from the organisation. Countries which have been suspended include Nigeria (1995), Pakistan (1999) and Fiji (2000 and 2006). As a last resort, a country can be expelled from the Commonwealth.

In 2002, Zimbabwe was suspended from the Commonwealth for 12 months after its presidential election was found by observers to be neither free nor fair. The election of Robert Mugabe was marred by violence and intimidation of opposition supporters. The following year Zimbabwe withdrew from the Commonwealth.

SUPPORTING SMALL AND VULNERABLE STARTS
STRENGTHENING TRADE
DEMOCRACY JUSTICE
HUMAN GOOD GOVERNANCE
RIGHTS CLIMATE CHANGE DEBT
THE ENVIRONMENT GENDER
HEALTH EQUALITY
ECONOMIC
EDUCATION DEVELOPMENT
EMPOWERING
YOUNG PEOPLE

▲ The aims of the Commonwealth

Homosexual rights

In 41 out of the 53 Commonwealth countries, homosexuality is illegal. Britain must make defending the rights of gay and lesbian people a key plank of its relations with other Commonwealth countries, according to the Speaker of the House of Commons, John Bercow.

"Four out of five Commonwealth countries criminalise homosexuality. Surely it is time for the Commonwealth to do more to support gay, lesbian, transsexual and bisexual people to ensure that they are not discriminated against, wherever they may live." John Bercow

In groups

"The Commonwealth has no right to interfere in the internal politics of member states."

"The Commonwealth should be prepared to act to bring about regime change if the government of a member country is undemocratic."

Say which of these two statements you agree with. Give your reasons.

In groups

"Britain should withhold aid from Commonwealth countries which deny homosexuals their rights." Discuss this view.

For your file

"Although its power and influence are ultimately limited, the Commonwealth serves a useful purpose."

Write a statement saying why you agree or disagree with this view.

Aim To understand what the United Nations is, what its aims are, and to examine its role in the world

The UN Charter

The United Nations (UN) was founded in 1945 by the countries that won the Second World War. It was designed to make sure that a war like the Second World War did not happen again. The UK is one of around 190 member countries who have signed the UN Charter which sets out the aims of the UN. These aims include:

- The development of friendly relations amongst nations.
- Co-operation on economic development.
- Co-operation on social and cultural development.
- Maintenance of international peace and security.
- Promotion of humanitarian issues that affect its member countries.

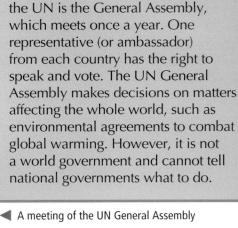

The UN General Assembly

The main policy-making body of the UN is the General Assembly, which meets once a year. One representative (or ambassador) from each country has the right to speak and vote. The UN General Assembly makes decisions on matters affecting the whole world, such as environmental agreements to combat global warming. However, it is not a world government and cannot tell national governments what to do.

◀ A meeting of the UN General Assembly

The UN Security Council

The UN Security Council was set up to settle disputes between countries and to try to preserve world peace. The Council has five permanent members – USA, UK, France, China and Russia. There are also 10 non-permanent members, elected for a two-year period. If a permanent member opposes a resolution, it has the power to veto the resolution. This has often made it difficult to get resolutions passed.

The role of the UN Security Council includes:

- discussing any situation where fighting has occurred or where there is a threat to international security. Issues discussed in 2014 included Israel's attack on Gaza.

- proposing actions and solutions, such as sanctions, political pressure or military intervention.

- sending UN peacekeeping forces to areas of conflict to try to prevent more fighting and to protect civilians.

On your own

Some people think that the number of permanent members of the UN Security Council should be increased to include, for example, a Muslim country and a country from Africa. There are also arguments for Japan, India, Germany and Brazil becoming permanent members. What do you think of these views? Should the Security Council be changed in order to reflect how the world has changed since 1945?

The UN Secretariat

The UN Secretariat, which is based in New York, oversees the administration and running of the UN. It is headed by the Secretary-General of the United Nations. Currently this is Ban Ki-moon of South Korea, elected in 2007.

The many different agencies and commissions below the Secretariat deal with world problems such as hunger, poverty, injustice, ill-health and illiteracy. Examples include the UN Commission for Human Rights, the UN High Commission for Refugees and the UN Commission for Children. The UK chooses to donate extra money to these particular commissions, as it believes these to be priority areas.

▲ A UN treatment centre dealing with the Ebola virus, 2014

The UN – helping to solve the world's problems

Homelessness

The UN High Commission for Refugees helps people who have left their homes either as a result of wars or natural disasters. It is estimated that since the 1950s this commission has helped 50 million refugees either to return to their homelands or to start a new life elsewhere.

Health

The World Health Organisation aims to promote health throughout the world. A major focus has been immunisation programmes, which have saved millions of lives by providing protection against diseases such as measles, tetanus, tuberculosis and whooping cough.

Environment

The UN Environment Programme aims to safeguard the global environment for future generations. It assists Less Economically Developed Countries to introduce environmentally sound practices, encouraging sustainable development.

Hunger

The World Food Programme aims to fight hunger wherever it occurs, providing food to refugees and emergency relief to people suffering from famine. It also gives support to long-term development projects to ensure people can grow their own food.

In pairs

"The UK is not a permanent member of the UN Security Council." True or false?

Draw up a quiz consisting of other true and false statements about the UN. Exchange your quiz with another pair and complete their quiz.

For your file

Prepare a fact sheet: "10 things you need to know about the UN."

Find out about two other UN bodies and draft a report of the work they do. Examples could include commissions that help the economic development of poorer countries, or eradication of illiteracy.

Wars, weapons and arms races

Aim To understand the arms trade, what weapons of mass destruction are and how they affect the world

What is the arms trade?

▼ Arms are bought and sold through trade fairs

The arms trade is the production and sale of all weapons and military equipment used by armies around the world. Almost £1000 billion a year is spent on arms, which represents around 3% of the world's production of all goods.

The UK is the world's fourth largest arms exporter after the USA, Russia and Germany. The government supports the arms trade in a number of ways: by giving grants to help the building of arms factories, by holding trade fairs and by helping arms firms to market their products.

Critics argue that the arms trade is damaging for three reasons:

1 It causes human misery through all the lives that are lost, people who are injured and the destruction that results from the use of weapons in wars.

2 It means that countries are more tempted to resolve situations by violence, rather than co-operating with one another.

3 It prevents money from being spent on other areas, such as education and health.

Arms races

An arms race occurs when one country starts to increase its military equipment and the size of its armed forces, then neighbouring countries get worried, so they in turn increase their military spending. As the problem spreads, countries spend more and more trying to outdo each other.

This has occurred in many regions of the world, particularly in parts of Africa. Arms races also took place between the USA and the USSR from 1960 to 1980, and between India and Pakistan in 2000.

In 2014, concerns about China's increased military spending fuelled an arms race in Asia, with India, Indonesia, Vietnam and Thailand all increasing their defence spending. In addition, there was also increased spending by countries in the Middle East, such as Saudi Arabia, due to concern about instability in the region.

In pairs

"Arms races are inevitable once one country in a region starts to increase its military spending."

Discuss why arms races occur and why you agree or disagree with this view.

An ethical arms trade

Supporters of the arms trade argue that if the UK does not sell arms to a country, another producer of arms will do so.

Opponents of the arms trade, such as CAAT (Campaign Against the Arms Trade), argue that what is needed is an ethical arms policy. This would mean that governments in countries with arms industries would refuse to sell arms to dictators and to countries where arms may be used aggressively, rather than as a means of defence.

Weapons of mass destruction

Weapons of mass destruction are weapons that can kill people in very large numbers. These weapons were invented or developed for widespread use in the 20th century. They are outlawed because of the extremely large number of people that they can kill indiscriminately. The list on the right shows some examples.

Biological weapons

These were the first type of weapon of mass destruction to be developed as they occur naturally. Biological weapons kill people by infecting them with deadly germs. Modern potential biological weapons include anthrax, botulism, and the Ebola virus.

Chemical weapons

Chemical weapons involve the use of toxic chemicals to kill or disable. They were first widely used in the First World War when chemicals like chlorine were added to mustard gas. As a result of the horrific injuries suffered by people during the First World War, the Geneva Convention of 1925 banned all chemical weapons. However, the Iraqi dictator Saddam Hussein used chemical weapons on his own people in the late 1980s in order to crush opposition to his rule. President Assad of Syria also used chemical weapons against his opponents in the Syrian civil war in 2013.

Nuclear weapons

These weapons were developed during the Second World War. In 1945 the USA dropped two nuclear bombs on the Japanese cities of Hiroshima and Nagasaki in order to force the Japanese to surrender. A nuclear explosion causes a huge fireball that kills everyone nearby and makes an area uninhabitable for many years to come, due to radioactive contamination.

New weapons of mass destruction

Following the events of 11th September 2001 in the USA (see page 79), terrorists proved that there were now new weapons of mass destruction. By using passenger aircraft as missiles, the terrorists were able to kill thousands of people as the chemical fuel in the planes exploded on impact with densely populated buildings.

In groups

"The UK should only manufacture arms for use by British forces or our allies."

"Until other countries agree to stop manufacturing and selling arms, we should go on doing so."

"The arms trade is immoral. We shouldn't sell arms to countries engaged in conflicts or where there are human rights abuses."

1 Explain why you agree or disagree with these statements.

2 On what ideas should an ethical arms policy be based? Give reasons for your views.

In pairs

Which do you think poses the greatest threat to humanity – biological, chemical or nuclear weapons? Give reasons for your views.

For your file

Research weapons of mass destruction on the Internet, then write an article about them and the threat from them.

What is terrorism?

Aim To discuss what terrorism is, what causes and maintains it, and how terrorism can be fought

What is terrorism and how is it caused?

Terrorists are people who want some sort of change. What makes them different from politicians and pressure groups is that they use violence to achieve their goals. They believe that nothing will happen if they don't commit acts of violence and that the end justifies the means.

Many terrorist groups want freedom and independence for a particular group or region. For example, the Basque terrorist group ETA, which planted bombs in Majorca in August 2009, wants independence for the Basque country (seven provinces on the western edge of the Pyrenees in northern Spain and southern France).

Other groups, such as Al-Qaeda and Islamic State want to change the balance of power in the world. They have declared a holy war against the USA, with the aim of causing chaos in the Middle East in order to reduce America's power and influence in the region.

◀ Members of Islamic State

What keeps terrorism going and how to stop it

Below are some reasons why terrorism continues and suggestions for ways to stop it.

1 THE CYCLE OF VIOLENCE One group decides to use violence to achieve its ends and another group retaliates. One way to stop the cycle of violence is the intervention of a third party to achieve conflict resolution. A ceasefire can be negotiated, but it may break down and the terrorist attacks restart.

2 STEREOTYPING Stereotyping is when people are identified only by the group they belong to. The assumption is that all people in that group behave in a certain way. An example of stereotyping is saying that in Northern Ireland all Protestants treat Catholics unfairly, or that all Catholics support the IRA. Stereotyping can be fought when people are treated as individuals and it is recognised that people behave in different ways.

3 INJUSTICE If one group can get away with crimes, its opposition will have no respect for the law. For example, if the government in Pakistan uses violence to stop its opponents from speaking out, it only helps the terrorists to justify their actions. A solution would be to create a rule of law requiring that everyone must be treated fairly.

4 WEAPONS If people have weapons, they are more likely to commit violence. Disarmament is a key way to reduce terrorism and violence.

5 ECONOMIC CONDITIONS People fight when they feel desperate. If there is economic growth and stability, people will have less reason to fight. There are fewer terrorist organisations in more economically developed countries that have a fair distribution of wealth.

In groups

Using the points above, discuss what you think is the main reason for terrorism continuing today. What is the best way to stop terrorism? Give reasons for your views.

Case study: New York 11th September 2001

On 11th September 2001, the terrorist group Al-Qaeda managed to hijack several planes inside the USA. Two of them were crashed in New York, destroying the World Trade Centre. Thousands of people died in the attacks.

Case study: London 7th July 2005

Three bombs exploded on tube trains simultaneously and another destroyed a nearby bus nearly an hour later. The suicide bombers killed 52 people and injured more than 700.

The war on terror

In response to the 11th September attack on New York, the US President George W Bush declared 'a war on terror'. The UK government, led by Tony Blair, supported this. The US and UK governments authorised the invasion of Afghanistan where the Al-Qaeda leader, Osama Bin Laden, was hiding. The Afghanistan Government was overthrown, but Bin Laden escaped.

In 2003, the USA linked the leader of Iraq, Saddam Hussein, to Al-Qaeda. It was also claimed that Iraq was hiding weapons of mass destruction (see page 77). Iraq was invaded by a group of countries led by the USA and the UK. However, the weapons of mass destruction have never been found, and the links between Saddam Hussein and Al-Qaeda were proved to be minimal.

Supporters of this military action say that the terrorists need to be taught a lesson. Also, they claim that terrorists no longer have the support of the governments of Afghanistan or Iraq.

Critics of the war say that all that the USA and the UK have done is to create a stronger ground for terrorism. This has led to continuing terrorist attacks in Iraq and the emergence of Islamic State.

For your file

Can terrorism ever be justified?

During the Second World War some groups undertook terrorist activity in order to fight Nazi atrocities. Do you think there is ever a case where terrorist activity can be justified? Write a short statement expressing your views.

In pairs

1 Were the USA and the UK right to respond to the events of 11th September by taking military action?

2 Say why you agree or disagree with each of the statements below.

"We were right to hunt down the terrorists. We were not right to start a war in Iraq. That has only encouraged more terrorists around the world."

"I wish we spent as much money on solving conflict and promoting peace as we did on the wars in Iraq and Afghanistan. Then, perhaps, there would be fewer terrorists in the first place."

Fighting terrorism

Aim To understand what Islamic State is and the difference between freedom fighters and terrorists

The civil war in Syria led to the emergence of a terrorist army, Islamic State (ISIS), which is prepared to kidnap and murder western aid workers and slaughter civilians in order to impose its rule in parts of Syria and Iraq. It claims it is fighting a holy war or jihad against the West. In response, a coalition of more than 20 countries, including Britain and led by the United States, began a bombing campaign against ISIS in 2014. The coalition is also providing support for the Kurdish and Iraqi armies fighting Islamic State on the ground.

notinmyname

The terrorist group occupying parts of Syria and Iraq call themselves Islamic State, but Muslims all over the world have spoken out against them saying that they do not represent Islam, which is a peaceful religion. Imams across the world have condemned them and Muslims have organised social media campaigns such as #notinmyname to make it clear that they do not support the actions of the terrorists. Young men and women from European countries, including Britain, who have been radicalised by extremists, have gone to join the terrorists in Syria.

"We know there are young men and women within our communities who have gone over and committed atrocities. What we are saying is that we value and cherish the values of peace, democracy and human rights. That's why we reject Islamic State. We also believe they're distorting the name of our faith. It's what we stand for as British women and Muslim women."

Sara Khan, co-founder of *Inspire*, a counter-extremism organisation

In groups

Young men and women from European countries, including Britain, who have been radicalised by extremists, have gone to join the terrorists in Syria.

Should British people suspected of holding extremist views and of wanting to join the jihadists have their passports confiscated?

Should British people who have been to Syria to fight but who want to return to the United Kingdom be denied entry or be detained on entry and questioned before a decision is made whether to allow them to return?

Should there be a law preventing people from expressing extremist views in support of jihad?

What effect has the bombing of Islamic State had? What else do you think governments should do to stop the advance of Islamic State?

Should British jihadists be charged with treason and given life sentences if they are found guilty?

Terrorists or Freedom Fighters?

Whether a person is a freedom fighter or a terrorist can depend on your point of view. The state of Israel was created in 1948 and takes up 78% of the land originally known as Palestine. Since 1967 Israel has occupied the other 22% which the Palestinians claim is their homeland. There have been violent clashes between the Israelis and the Palestinians in the uprisings or intifada that took place between 1987–1993 and 2000–2003. Attempts to negotiate a peace settlement continue, but so too does the conflict between the Israelis and Palestinians which led to the Israeli bombardment of Gaza in 2014, resulting in over 2000 deaths.

▲ Protests against the bombing of Gaza take place worldwide

The Israelis' aim was to destroy tunnels which had been built on the border between Gaza and Israel and used by the militant Palestinian group Hamas to store weapons, shield its supporters and to launch attacks on Israel. Hamas has also launched rocket attacks and sent suicide bombers into Israel.

From the Israeli point of view, members of Hamas and other Palestinian militant groups are terrorists who threaten Israeli civilians. They are also regarded as terrorists by the USA, Canada, Australia and by the United Kingdom and the other members of the EU. From the Palestinian point of view they are fighting for freedom. They are also regarded as freedom fighters by Iran, Russia, Turkey, China and some Arab states.

▲ The result of an Israeli bombing raid on Gaza, 2014

The IRA

The Provisional IRA was a paramilitary organisation which carried out a series of bombings in Northern Ireland and in England between 1969, when it was formed, and 1998. It also attacked British forces stationed in Northern Ireland and police officers in the Ulster Constabulary. Its aim was to free Northern Ireland from British rule. It was opposed by loyalist paramilitary groups who attacked IRA targets in defence of the Union.

Following the Good Friday agreement in 1998, the Provisional IRA agreed to disarm. However, groups of dissidents, calling themselves the Real IRA and the Continuity IRA have continued to carry out attacks in Northern Ireland.

The Provisional IRA were labelled terrorists for their bombing campaigns and their attacks by the British media, but supporters regarded them as people fighting for a united Ireland.

In groups

"Members of Hamas are terrorists, not freedom fighters." Do you agree with this view? Or are they merely protecting themselves from Israeli state-sponsored terrorism? Give reasons for your views.

81

Environmental issues

Aim To explore sustainable development and the main ways it could be applied around the world

The economy and the environment

Since the industrial revolution started in the UK in the 1700s, economic development around the world has accelerated. As a result, this has often meant that the environment has not been protected when developments have occurred. This means there are now several human-made threats to our environment occurring across the world. These include:

Global warming: Gases released by burning fossil fuels mean that more carbon dioxide gas (CO_2) is now present in the Earth's atmosphere. This traps more of the sun's energy, causing the planet to heat up. This leads to a rise in sea levels, extensive flooding, and extreme weather conditions.

Pollution: More of our natural environment is becoming polluted with chemicals from human activities, such as industry. Air pollution from traffic is one of the main causes of asthma in the UK today. Meanwhile, chemicals entering our water cause acid rain that is damaging trees and forests, and contributes to species extinction.

Species extinction: More of the natural environment is destroyed when forests are cut down, roads created, and more houses built. This leaves less natural land for other living creatures, leading to a loss of biodiversity (the number of different living species in an area). In some cases, plants and animals die out. This is known as species extinction. It is estimated that half of all life living on Earth has died since the 1960s.

▼ The tiger faces extinction as more of its natural environment is destroyed

Sustainable development

Sustainable development is different from economic development. This is because development still occurs, but only when it does not damage the environment. Sustainable development requires three main factors to be considered:

1 That scarce natural resources are not wasted and natural alternatives are used where possible.

2 That the environment is not damaged, now or in the future.

3 That it is actually achievable in the long term. For example, if we were all to stop driving cars overnight, we would need an alternative form of transport.

In groups

Which of the above three human-made problems poses the most threat to the environment in the UK? What do you think we can do to help the situation? Give reasons for your views.

environmental issues

Sustainable solutions around the world

Sustainable development needs to take place on a global scale in order to make a real difference. There are three main areas where this is needed:

1 Energy consumption: Much of our energy consumption comes from burning scarce natural resources, such as wood in less economically developed countries, and oil, coal and gas in more economically developed countries.

One solution in more developed countries has been to use nuclear energy. This is cheap and does not produce any gases that contribute to global warming. However, nuclear energy produces waste material that remains dangerous because it is radioactive for hundreds of years.

Two other alternatives are wind and wave power. Turbines are used to harvest natural energy from the wind and from the waves in the sea.

2 Food consumption: Vast amounts of food are consumed across the world. However, the intensive growing of crops to meet this demand often damages the soil. The use of pesticides to increase the amount of food grown can increase chemical pollution.

One solution has been to develop genetically modified (GM) crops that use less pesticide. Supporters of GM crops say they are environmentally friendly. However, critics argue that the long-term effects of GM crops are not known.

3 Protecting natural resources: Wood is a scare natural resource that is being used up rapidly around the planet. Cutting down trees for wood leads to deforestation, particularly in places like South America. This leads to a loss of biodiversity, and increases species extinction and global warming.

One solution is sustainable forestry – replanting trees to replace those that are cut down. However, new trees can take years to grow.

In pairs

Decide on four reasons why you support or oppose (a) the development of a wind farm on a hillside near your home and (b) a farmer growing GM crops in fields near where you live.

Sustainable development in developed and less economically developed countries

By economically developing to fight poverty, countries often over-exploit their natural resources. India's and China's rapid development in recent decades has also increased their energy consumption dramatically and at the same time increased pollution.

More developed countries, such as the USA and UK, argue that any development needs to be sustainable. However, critics say that more developed countries should first clean up their own acts. For example, the USA uses 40% of the world's energy resources. The biggest change that could therefore be made to the environment would be the USA reducing its energy consumption.

For your file

"It is hypocritical of us to tell less economically developed countries that they have to stick to sustainable development, when more developed countries don't clean up their own acts."

"We should be doing more to help less economically developed countries undertake sustainable development. After all, it's in our interests as well as theirs."

Explain what sustainable development means and say why you agree or disagree with these two statements.

Taking action to protect the environment

Aim To understand what your water footprint is and to explore ways of taking action to reduce your consumption of natural resources

Reducing your water footprint

"Water covers two-thirds of the Earth's surface, yet it has never been more precious. A UN report has predicted that severe water shortages would affect 4 billion people by 2050."

www.wwf.org.uk

FACTS AND FIGURES

- To produce one cup of black coffee without sugar requires 140 litres of water to grow the beans, transport them and serve the coffee in the cup.

- Producing a slice of white bread involves only 40 litres of water, but a burger requires 2,400 litres.

- In the UK, the average annual water footprint is 1,695 cubic metres per person, compared to 2,900 cubic metres per person in the USA. About 62% of the UK water footprint is related to the consumption of imported products.

In groups

1 "Products should have labels telling consumers how much water it requires to produce them." Do you think this would influence what consumers buy?

2 Explain what a water footprint is. List suggestions of what individuals could do to reduce their water footprints, e.g. buy homegrown foods rather than imported foods.

3 The average daily direct use of water in the house is 150 litres per person. Suggest how you might cut down your water usage.

For your file

Find out more about world water scarcity and water footprints from websites such as www.wwf.org.uk and www.waterfootprint.org. Write an article for a teenage magazine entitled: "Why your water footprint matters."

In pairs

Imagine you had to design a building in your local area. List the features that you would include to make it environmentally friendly.

Reducing rubbish

In the UK, large amounts of rubbish are buried in the ground, or burnt, which causes air pollution. A key issue is, therefore, how much waste we need to recycle. Different cities around the world have come up with different solutions:

In Oxford, there are separate street bins for three types of rubbish in the city centre. You have to put glass and cans in one bin, paper in another, and the remaining rubbish in the third. This makes it easier for the council to recycle the rubbish.

In Toronto, Canada, it is illegal to throw away glass bottles that could be recycled. This encourages people to take their bottles to a bottle bank, where they can be recycled.

▲ A battery-powered electric car charging from a 'Juice Point'

Reducing energy consumption

Reducing the amount of energy we use means that we reduce pollution caused by generating energy. These are some of the methods that have been used internationally to reduce the amount of energy used:

In Australia, new apartment blocks have solar power to provide them with hot water. This means that electricity and gas bills are reduced, as solar power is a form of sustainable energy.

In Chicago, buildings have rooftop gardens. These keep the heat off the building, thus reducing electricity required for air conditioning. The plants in these gardens also reduce CO_2 gases.

In London, using battery-powered vehicles is encouraged. These create no noise and no air pollution. The battery-powered vehicles can only travel up to 40mph, which is faster than most London traffic!

In pairs

1 What sort of recycling facilities exist in your local area? Do you think it should be illegal not to recycle your rubbish? Give reasons for your views.

2 Should there be a 'bin tax'? Should households have to pay for each tonne of rubbish they produce? Give reasons for your views.

For your file

Research and write a short report about what your local council is doing to solve the environmental problems in your area.

Campaigning for change

Aim To understand what international pressure groups are, what issues they campaign on, and what campaign methods they use

What are international pressure groups?

International pressure groups campaign on global issues such as world peace, tackling world poverty, or fighting the spread of AIDS.

Some international pressure groups campaign on a range of different but connected issues. For example, the international pressure group Greenpeace looks at everything that affects the environment on a global scale.

In addition to targeting national governments to try to influence their policies, international pressure groups target international institutions. These can represent groups of countries, for instance the European Union (EU) or the Organisation of Petroleum Exporting Countries (OPEC) which produce most of the world's oil, or organisations such as the World Bank or the International Monetary Fund (IMF) which make decisions that affect the world's economy.

International pressure groups also target big businesses, in particular multinational corporations, such as Nike, McDonalds or BP. These companies are spread over many countries and wield enormous economic power.

International pressure group Greenpeace campaigns on a global scale

The antiglobalisation movement

Sometimes, international pressure groups may come together to form a 'coalition' – working together to try to achieve a common aim.

An example of a coalition is the antiglobalisation movement, which protests against the economic, social and environmental damage that world economic growth causes around the world today. The coalition includes environmental pressure groups, some Trades Unions, left-wing pressure groups and anarchists (people who are opposed to authority, such as governments).

Role play

Imagine that a friend asks you to join an antiglobalisation protest. Role-play the scene in which they ask you to take part. Do you agree? Why?

On your own

Choose one of the 12 international pressure groups mentioned on the next page. Research their current campaigns and design a poster to be used in one of their campaigns. What slogan will you use? What image will you use?

International pressure group issues

Here is a list of the four main areas in which international pressure groups are campaigning today, with examples.

Economic issues

These include:

1 Reducing world poverty. In particular, reducing the poverty of some less developed countries where people live on less than 60p a day. International pressure group: War on Want

2 Eliminating Third World debt, so that Third World countries are not continually paying back interest on outstanding money that they have borrowed. International pressure group: World Development Movement (WDM)

3 Fair trade instead of free trade. This is where goods are produced without workers being exploited. International pressure group: The Fairtrade Foundation

Conflict issues

Conflict issues arise out of wars and conflicts around the world today. Issues campaigned on include:

4 The arms trade. Many international pressure groups argue that governments should spend less on arms and more on other areas. International pressure group: Campaign Against the Arms Trade (CAAT)

5 Nuclear weapons. A number of international pressure groups believe that nuclear weapons are dangerous and should be banned and destroyed. International pressure group: Campaign for Nuclear Disarmament (CND)

6 Landmines. When a war is over, landmines can be left, causing death and serious injury for many years afterwards. International pressure group: Oxfam

Environmental issues

These are all interlinked, as one environmental issue often connects to another.

7 Access to clean water. Millions of people currently live without access to a clean water supply. International pressure group: Water Aid

8 Global warming. The threat of global warming can lead to loss of land, changing weather patterns, and displacement of people. International pressure group: Friends of the Earth

9 Species extinction. This is when a particular animal dies out and becomes extinct. On a large scale, extinction has serious consequences. For example, if many species of fish become extinct, an important food supply is lost. International pressure group: World Wildlife Fund (WWF)

Social issues

Social issues affect the way that we choose to live. Examples of important social issues include:

10 Discrimination. Many international human rights pressure groups exist to fight for human rights issues and against discrimination, including sexism, racism and homophobia. International pressure group: Amnesty International

11 Ensuring the rights of children. As a vulnerable group, children are more likely to be exploited. Some international pressure groups exist specifically to promote and protect the rights of children. International pressure groups: the Red Cross and the Red Crescent

12 Political reform. Other international pressure groups exist to promote political reform to ensure that there is freedom of speech and that governments do not abuse their powers. International pressure group: Kofi Annan Foundation

In pairs

Rank the 12 examples of international pressure group issues given above in order of importance, starting with the most important and finishing with the least. Share your top three with the rest of the class.

For your file

Imagine you win £100 to donate to an international pressure group of your choice. Explain which organisation you would give it to and why.

Campaigning for change

Aim To understand how international pressure groups campaign and to explore ways of getting involved

Getting the message across

Local and national pressure groups use a range of methods to get their message across. These include drawing up petitions, sending mailings, distributing leaflets, running advertising campaigns, and lobbying politicians. They also use the media, for example by sending out press releases to gain publicity for events such as demonstrations.

International pressure groups use similar methods. However, due to the size of the audiences they are trying to influence, they often have larger-scale and more powerful campaign techniques.

Protest days

In order to highlight their cause, an international pressure group may hold a special day to draw attention to it. An example is International AIDS day, which seeks to draw attention to the suffering of people who have AIDS or who are HIV-positive.

Lengthy, co-ordinated campaigns

Because of their size, international pressure groups can run campaigns that are lengthy and involve a sizeable number of people. When groups of protesters campaign in several cities, people are forced to take notice.

High profile media stunts

Sometimes pressure groups feel that the only way to get attention is to do something outrageous. Such stunts may be expensive, but if they attract enough attention worldwide, it is worth it. For example, in 2003 Greenpeace launched boats to intercept vessels carrying nuclear waste.

Civil disobedience

Some international pressure groups choose to use illegal action to get their message across. Often, these actions break the law, but they do not physically harm anybody. This is known as 'civil disobedience'.

An example of this is when, under a dictatorship or in conflict zones, people break the law to gather evidence of human rights abuses. For instance, during the Second Gulf War in 2003–4, peace activists broke through Israeli security in order to gather evidence of alleged atrocities against the Palestinians.

▲ Protest days can be an effective way to draw attention to issues

In groups

Discuss the views below.

"The ends do not justify the means. You cannot break the law just to get your point across."

"If no-one gets hurt, why shouldn't people make an informed decision to break the law? But they should be willing to accept the punishment that goes with it."

Getting involved

"I joined CAAT (Campaign Against the Arms Trade) because I'm concerned about landmines and the way they kill people and ruin their lives by maiming them, even after a conflict has ended.

I saw this documentary on TV about an African country. The people had all come back to their village but there were lots of places they couldn't go because of landmines. One day a teenage boy stepped on a mine and it blew his leg off.

I support CAAT because they campaign to get the manufacture of landmines banned completely." Mel

"I decided to support Water Aid for a number of reasons, not only because they want to make sure that people in poorer countries don't have to walk several kilometres to get their water, but also because they aim to provide everyone in the world with clean water.

I read about the diseases that can be caught if all you have to drink is dirty water that's been polluted by sewage. So I decided Water Aid was the pressure group I wanted to support." Harid

Case study: working in Africa

Working as a volunteer passes on valuable skills

When Laura was 18, she volunteered to spend her gap year working in a school in Africa before she trained to be a teacher:

"I was very keen to spend a gap year abroad. However, when I applied to do voluntary service in Africa, they told me that my contribution would be much more valuable if I was already a trained teacher. They explained that what was needed most were trained people with the skills they could pass on to local people, rather than unskilled volunteers. So I trained as a teacher and then spent a year in Africa.

It was a rewarding, if sometimes harrowing, experience. In Britain we take so much for granted. In the area where I worked in Africa, the school didn't have the equipment or supplies that we have and the number of people who wanted to learn was overwhelming. But the staff were wonderful and I learned a lot from the students. It's altered my whole way of looking at things."

In pairs

Which international issues concern you most? Which international pressure group or groups would be your first choice to support?

For your file

Choose an international issue that concerns you. Imagine that you work for a pressure group and draft a letter asking people for their support on that issue.

In pairs

1 Discuss what Laura says about why her voluntary service was so rewarding.

2 Would you ever consider doing voluntary work abroad? If so, what would you like to do? Who would you like to help? Give reasons for your answers.

Volunteering

Aim To examine what volunteering involves and how it can benefit you and your local community

What is volunteering?

A volunteer is someone who does a task or job for free. Volunteering can be done over any period of time, anywhere. Some people may volunteer to pick litter up in their local park for an afternoon. Others may volunteer to help out at their local day centre for older people once a week for a month. Some people may choose to help out in their local charity shop every Saturday during a gap year.

People volunteer for many different reasons. Usually they want to contribute something to their local community. However, there are also several benefits for the volunteer. These include:

- developing transferable skills that can be used in other jobs
- filling up free time
- receiving training that will help them in their career
- gaining practical on-the-job experience
- pursuing a particular form of work that they enjoy
- getting job satisfaction from a task well done.

Getting involved

■ Helping other young people
"I volunteered to help with a scheme whereby we befriend a young person with a disability and go on trips with them."

■ Improving facilities for young people locally
"I got involved helping to build an extension to our youth centre. In a way, it was like doing work experience and I learned a lot."

■ Helping older people
"Twice a week after school I visit an old lady who lives on her own. It's like having another great-grandma."

■ Looking after the environment
"I spent several Saturdays working as part of a team cleaning up a riverbank. I learned a lot about the sort of rubbish that pollutes rivers and my team leader said he'd give me a reference."

In groups

Do you know anyone who has done any voluntary work? What do you think their reasons for doing voluntary work were? Why might you want to do voluntary work in the future?

In pairs

Discuss the different types of voluntary work (see left). Talk about how each type benefits the community and what the young volunteers get from doing voluntary work.

Make a Difference Day is held on the last Saturday of October each year. It is organised by Community Service Volunteers (CSV), a charity that seeks to involve people in short- or long-term voluntary projects.

The idea of CSV Make a Difference Day is that people volunteer to give up some of their time – either a morning, an afternoon or a whole day – to take part in a project to help others. It gives people a chance to work together to do something that will benefit the community.

How to identify your project

- Always remember, you know your own area best. Look around you and ask yourself – what could I do to make a difference?

- Think about issues that concern you. You might be concerned about the state of the environment, for example, about a place that is used for fly-tipping, or a neglected area where shrubs or trees could be planted. Or there might be a local care home for older people where you could befriend an older person who has no visitors.

- Ask your neighbours and friends in the area. What issues are they concerned about? Where do they think action is needed? Who is in need of a helping hand?

- Consult local community leaders. Is there an existing project that you could get involved in?

- Think about the skills that you have and how you could use them to help other people.

- Think about organisations that you might be able to help. The list of organisations that you might involve in your activity is enormous e.g. local nurseries, wildlife trusts, youth or community centres, hospices, hospitals and care homes.

Source: adapted from *CSV Make a Difference Day Handbook*

In groups

Share your ideas for projects in a class discussion, then plan and carry out a class Make a Difference Day event.

In pairs

Imagine that your group has decided to take part in this year's CSV Make a Difference Day campaign. Use the suggestions (on the next page) to help you to identify a project.

For your file

Find out about successful Make a Difference Day events that have been held in the past and about plans for this year's Make a Difference Day from websites, such as www.csv.org. Use the information to draft a statement to present to the school council arguing that the school should become involved in this year's Make a Difference Day scheme.

Getting involved in a community project

Aim To explore how to choose, get involved in and complete a community volunteer project

Meeting the needs of the local community

Most volunteer projects are undertaken in order to directly benefit the local community in some way. A successful voluntary project:

- meets the needs of the local community
- meets the needs of the volunteers
- is carefully managed so that both needs are realistic and achievable.

There are two ways of identifying what community issues would benefit from a voluntary project. One is to simply walk round and see what needs doing in your local area. Is there much graffiti? Are there enough facilities for young people?

A second approach is to conduct a survey of people to find out what they think needs doing. This will give you a clear idea of what local people think the priorities are for their area. This is important – if you pick an issue that people think is a priority, you'll get more volunteers to help you with your project.

Resources needed

The following resources are needed to make a voluntary project work:

1 **Human resources**
Volunteers, and sometimes specialist help. Find volunteers through holding meetings or placing an advert. Local media, such as the local newspaper or radio station, may be willing to help for free.

2 **Financial resources**
Enough money to fund the project. This could be donated, for example, through sponsorship by a local business, or money available from a charity, the local council, or the government.

3 **Raw materials**
These may be available from the school, a local business, or a local charity.

Getting involved

These are some of the voluntary projects carried out by schools throughout the UK.

- Developing a mentor project, where older pupils help younger ones with a variety of issues, whether it's tackling bullying at school, developing reading skills, or staying healthy.
- Setting aside an area of the school to be used as an environmental centre, either by planting flowers or creating a pond to increase biodiversity (the number of different living creatures in an area).
- Developing an after-school work club to maximise work experience opportunities locally and train young people, through a partnership between local businesses and students.

 **In pairs**

Which of the voluntary projects on the left do you think would be most beneficial to your school? Why? Suggest other projects that would be of benefit (a) to the school and (b) to the local area.

For your file

Draft a questionnaire to survey what local people see as the needs of the community. Then develop a project to meet one of those needs.

Planning a voluntary project

Once you have decided what resources you need, you then need to plan your project in detail. This involves:

- breaking down your project into manageable stages
- developing a clear timetable
- deciding how you will measure the success of your project.

Case study: organising a petition for a skate park

Marcy and Rafiq think their neighbourhood needs more facilities for young people. They decide to get up a petition to the council to build a skate park on the local recreation ground and to organise a meeting to launch the petition. Joe, Stuart and Emma are also enthusiastic about the idea, so the group decides to go ahead with the project.

Manageable stages

Marcy decides to break the project down into manageable stages and gives a role to each of the other volunteers:

1 Emma is to write out the petition and to make copies of it for people to sign.
2 Joe is to design posters about the launch and, with Rafiq, to produce an A4 sheet saying why the skate park is needed, which will be handed out at the launch.
3 Rafiq is to find out when they can have a room either at school or in the community centre to launch the petition.
4 Stuart is put in charge of contacting the media, including writing press releases to the local paper and trying to get a radio interview.
5 Marcy's role is that of project manager. She will be checking that everyone else is doing his or her job, and covering in case anyone is ill or too busy.

Developing a clear timetable

As project manager, Marcy develops, and is in charge of, a timetable for the project.

Week 1:
Rafiq to fix a date, time and place for the launch.

Week 2:
By the end of the week, Emma will have drafted the petition, Joe designed the posters and, with Rafiq, drafted the handout for the meeting. Stuart will have contacted the media.

Week 3:
Posters to be put up. Copies of the petition and the handout to be made.

Week 4:
Marcy to check that everything is ready, before holding the launch in Week 5.

Weeks 6 and 7:
Collect signatures and present the petition in Week 8.

For your file

Measure the success of your project by carrying out another survey and analysing the feedback to identify what went right and what went wrong.

19 Managing your money

Borrowing and buying on credit

Aim To explore the world of borrowing, credit and debt, so as to be able to make informed and prudent choices when thinking about borrowing money

Borrowing money

Banks don't let people under 18 years of age borrow money, but when you turn 18 the chances are you'll be offered credit cards and loans.

Borrowing means buying now and paying later. When you borrow, you enter into a contract: the lender agrees to give you a lump sum now, and you agree to make regular payments (usually once a month) to pay back the lump sum. What's in it for the lender? They charge you interest on the amount of the loan.

Interest is expressed as an annual percentage rate (APR), which means you pay a certain percentage a year in addition to the amount of the loan. For example, if you borrowed £200 at an APR of 15% and agreed to pay it back after a year, you would pay £30 interest as well as the £200 loan.

Different ways to borrow

Method of borrowing	Advantages	Disadvantages
Credit cards	A good way of getting an interest-free loan if you pay off the outstanding balance each month.	One of the worst ways of borrowing in the long term if you are only able to pay off a small amount of what you owe each month.
Overdraft	Can be a cheap, flexible way to help with temporary cash-flow problems; some accounts even allow you to go overdrawn without paying fees and interest.	An expensive way of borrowing if it's not arranged with the bank in advance. Not suitable for long-term borrowing.
Bank loan	A good way of paying for long-term borrowing, as it allows you to plan your finances.	Not very flexible and watch out for the interest rates on the loan!
Hire purchase	Allows you to pay off a purchase over a long period of time in a planned way.	An expensive way of borrowing, and you don't own the goods until you have paid off the whole loan.

▲ A demonstration against payday loan company Wonga

BORROWING TIPS

1 Only borrow if you really need the item or service and you've worked out how you will repay the money.

2 Don't ignore loan repayments or credit card bills just because you can't afford to pay them. This will make your debt even worse.

3 If your debts are out of hand, get help immediately. See your bank or the Citizens Advice Bureau.

WHY PAYDAY LOANS ARE DANGEROUS

The bottom line is payday loans are a vicious circle of indebtedness. The companies prey on those who can least afford the fees and many customers are encouraged to keep getting further into debt by 'rolling over' (extending) the loans.

There is no accountability in terms of preventing customers from digging deeper holes for themselves. Unlike financial institutions that limit borrowers, payday loan customers are on a continual merry-go-round.

The reality is that many people do not stop at using the service once and then walking away. It becomes a way of making ends meet. But things never even out, they just get worse.

Source: adapted from The Payday Loans Homepage

THE DEBT TRAP

Many payday lenders target students. It can be tempting if you see an advert saying £1000 can be in your account within an hour. However, there are incredibly high interest rates on payday loans; some as high as 5,853%! You can find yourself trapped in a circle of debt that it is almost impossible to escape from.

On your own

Find out what a credit union is. How do credit unions help people who need to take out a loan?

In groups

1 "Payday lenders are loan sharks. To be avoided at all costs." Louis (18) – Discuss this view.

2 You need to borrow £200 to buy the books you need for your college course and for a bicycle so that you can get yourself to and from college without having to pay for a student bus pass. How would you borrow the money?

For your file

"I'm about to go to college for three years. I keep getting letters offering me credit cards and I'm quite tempted, especially by the ones that offer free gifts. What should I do?" Trefor, 18

Draft a reply to Trefor.

Work and pay

Aim To understand the financial aspects of starting work

How do I get paid?

Whether you are doing a part-time job in a shop, or your first full-time job after leaving school, you will find there are various ways in which you may be paid for your work (see the table on the right).

How you may be paid

Wage	Money that is paid daily, weekly, or monthly for work done. There is a national minimum wage that employers must pay to their employees (workers).
Salary	A whole year's pay (usually paid monthly).
Overtime	Money paid for working more hours than in your contract. This is often paid at a higher hourly rate.
Commission	Money paid for work done, either instead of a wage or in addition to a wage. Someone selling gym equipment may get £300 per week plus a commission of 3% of the total of all her sales that week.

Your payslip

National Insurance number: everyone gets a National Insurance (NI) number when they are 16. It is used for identification for work and training, or when claiming benefits.

Income tax: a percentage of your earnings goes to the Inland Revenue (the government) to pay for education, transport, etc. If you are a single person, the first £10,000 of your salary is free of tax.

Gross pay: your total monthly pay before any deductions (see right).

Pension scheme contribution: NI contributions only fund a small state pension, so many people decide to put some money aside each month into a separate pension scheme, which may be offered by your employer. The amount would be shown here.

National Insurance (NI) contribution: a percentage of your earnings helps to pay for government social services, such as health and state pensions. What you pay is used to calculate the amount of pension you will receive when you retire.

MIDCHESTER
COUNTY COUNCIL
EMPLOYEE NUMBER: 115847
NI NUMBER: HD 42 45 62 H
TAX CODE: 474L

PAY ADVICE:
MR BILL PAYER
DATE: 31.05.15
TAX MONTH: 2

	GROSS PAY	DEDUCTIONS		NET PAY
SALARY	1000	TAX	40.00	
		NI	39.00	
		PENSION	20.00	
TOTALS	1000		99.00	901.00

YEAR TO DATE
GROSS SALARY 2000.00
TAX 80.00
NI 78.00
PENSION 40.00

Net pay: the total amount of pay you take home after all the deductions.

Source: *Starting Work*, Citizenship Foundation

In pairs

Discuss the statement on the right. Do you agree with it? Give reasons for your views.

"I don't agree with paying tax and National Insurance on my earnings. I think people should take home every penny they earn."

Working teens – Q&A

What age can I work? You can't work until you are 13, unless you are doing modelling, TV or theatre work, when a performance licence has to be issued by the local authority.

What work can I do? From 13, teenagers can do 'light' work, e.g. working in local shops, hairdressers or cafés, doing paper rounds, car washing etc. You can't be involved in food preparation, though.

How much work can I do? During term time you can work up to 12 hours a week. This includes the maximum two hours on school days and on Sundays and up to five hours on Saturdays, or eight hours on Saturdays for 15- to 16-year olds. During school holidays 15- to 16-year-olds can work up to 35 hours a week; with a maximum eight hours a day and up to two hours work on Sundays.

And what about when I have left school?
Once you reach the minimum school leaving age – i.e. until the last Friday in June within the academic year of your 16th birthday – you can apply for your national insurance number and work full time.

Does the minimum wage apply? If you are 18 to 20, the minimum wage is £5.13 per hour. Young workers aged 16 to 17 are entitled to at least £3.79 per hour.

Minimum wage for young people is pathetic

£3.79 – is that some kind of sick joke? I know this rate is for the under 18s, and frankly some people that age are really just a waste of time and money in the workplace. But then there are others who are real hard workers and deserve the same rate as the over 21s (£6.50). Sadly, most companies are greedy and are more interested in keeping the profit for themselves, so these young workers are very unlikely to get a pay rise. If they complain then they'll be out on their ear and replaced by some other youngster. Well that's how business works, right?

The government should seriously rethink the whole minimum wage policy as it appears to me to be most unfair. I would even go as far as to say it's a blatant case of ageism. I think it's high time the minimum wage was set to be equal across the board, one rate of pay for all workers regardless of age.

Source: Equality for all / www.weeklygripe.co.uk

In groups

1 Make a list of jobs that you have already done, or that your brothers and sisters have done. How much do you/they earn? How close is this to the minimum wage? How long do you/they work for? Discuss your findings with the class.

2 Do you agree with the views expressed in the article "Minimum wage for young people is pathetic"? Give your reasons.

On your own

Look at some job adverts in your local paper and find out about how the workers are paid. Look at whether overtime or commission is available, and how much and how often an employee is paid.

For your file

"I've been offered some part-time work serving behind the counter in a local fast food outlet. They want me to do Saturdays from 9am to 7pm, with an hour off for lunch and three hours after school on Wednesdays from 4.30 to 7.30 p.m. The pay is £3.00 an hour – is this a reasonable deal or should they be giving me the minimum wage?"
Christine, 16

Draft a reply to Christine.

Aim to explore how the economy functions

What is the economy?

The economy of a country is the production and exchange of goods and services. Money is usually used to pay for this. The UK economy is made up of all the businesses that operate and trade in the UK.

Each of us deals with a wide variety of different businesses each day. You get up and switch on the light – somebody provides the electricity. You have a shower – somebody provides the water. You have breakfast – somebody provides the orange juice, the toast, and the toaster.

All these businesses are either manufacturing industries (they make things) or service industries (they provide services). The bus driver who takes you to school is providing a service, as is your teacher. When you use the Internet, you are also being provided with a service.

In recent years, the number of people working in manufacturing industries has fallen, while the number of people working in service industries has risen.

The size of the economy can be measured by adding up the value of all the goods and services produced in a year. This is known as the "Gross National Product" or GNP of a country. By dividing this by the number of people in a country, we can get an accurate measurement of the country's wealth per person. This is known as the average GNP per person.

On your own

On your own, make a list of all the different products and services you have used today. Which have you used more of – products or services? Then, with a partner, compare your lists. How similar are they? Are you surprised by the length of the list?

The profit cycle

Most businesses have to make a profit in order to survive. By making a large profit, a business can have enough money to be able to reinvest some of it in the business to expand it and produce more goods or services. This should lead to greater profits in the future.

The profit is the difference between how much it costs to make a product or provide a service, and how much income you receive from selling it. This can be shown in the profit cycle (see below).

Buy raw materials needed to make a product or provide a service

Reinvest

Create product or service

MAKE PROFIT

Gain income

Sell product or service

▼ The manufacturing sector of the economy has decreased in size over the last 60 years

Economic systems

There are three types of economic system:

- A free market economy is a system in which decisions about what goods and services to produce, how to produce them and how they are distributed are taken by individuals and firms, free of government interference.
- A planned economy, also known as a command economy, is a system in which the state or government controls what is produced and makes all the decisions about how the goods and services are distributed.
- A mixed economy is one in which there are features of both a free market economy and a planned economy.

Those in favour of the planned economy argue that the government is best placed to meet the needs of all the people in a particular society. Examples of planned economies were the USSR (the former Union of Soviet Socialist Republics) under communism and, until recently, communist China.

Those in favour of the free market economy argue that consumers get what they want to have produced, while producers supply it at a profit whereas central planning wastes resources.

In reality, most societies operate some form of mixed economy.

The UK
– A mixed economy

In the UK, we have a mixed economy. Most decisions are made by the market, according to the laws of demand and supply. Producers supply what consumers demand. For example, when you buy goods at a supermarket you vote with your money for the goods that you want to buy. However, some decisions are made by the government, for example those relating to road building, school and hospital construction, or the supply of medicines in hospitals.

In the UK the emphasis is on letting the market make most decisions because of its high level of efficiency in responding to customer preferences. However, there are some decisions that must be made by the government on behalf of society, for example decisions about military spending, and public education.

Source: adapted from www.thetimes100.co.uk

 In pairs

Say whether these statements are true or false.

- In a command system decision-making is centralised.
- In the UK economy most decisions are made by the market.
- The laws of supply and demand decide what is produced in a command economy.
- Most societies have a free market economy.

In groups

Discuss the difference between a free market economy and a planned economy. What is the UK's economic system?

Aim To understand how the government manages the economy and how it collects and spends money

Managing the economy

The government's main aim is to control the amount the economy grows. In order to achieve steady economic growth, the government has to balance two factors – inflation and unemployment.

Inflation

Inflation is the amount prices rise each year. Fighting inflation is important because many people have fixed incomes. As prices rise, the amount they earn stays fixed. This means that during times when prices rise rapidly – when inflation is high – these people lose out.

Unemployment

This is a measure of the number of people of working age who do not have a job. There is a natural amount of unemployment in any economy – usually about 5% of the workforce, as people move between jobs. Fighting unemployment is important, as it reduces poverty. It also reduces crime and the amount of money the government has to pay to people out of work to help them survive. The latter is known as unemployment benefit.

Growth and recession

Sometimes, the economy will contract. When this happens for two three-month periods in a row, it is known as a recession. Recessions have occurred in the UK economy in the early 1980s, the early 1990s, and from 2008 to 2010.

Many different things can cause a recession. The recession in the early 1980s was caused by a shortage of oil in the world. The most recent recession was caused by banks taking too many risks in the US property market.

Deflation

Sometimes in a recession prices can start to fall. This is called deflation. This is dangerous because people stop buying things while they wait for them to become cheaper. This can make a recession worse.

Managing the recession

In order to stop more people becoming unemployed, the government has to try to successfully manage the recession. One way of doing this is by spending lots of government money. This increases demand for products and services, thus helping firms survive the recession. This policy is favoured by the Labour Party.

However, the money spent has to come from somewhere. Unless it raises taxes, a government will have to borrow more money to finance its spending. This means the public sector borrowing requirement will rise, leaving a debt for the long term. Managing this debt in the recession, by cutting the amount of government spending, is favoured by the Conservative Party.

In groups

Which do you think is more important – spending our way out of the recession, or cutting the public debt? Why? Give reasons for your views.

▼ Many retailers go out of business during a recession

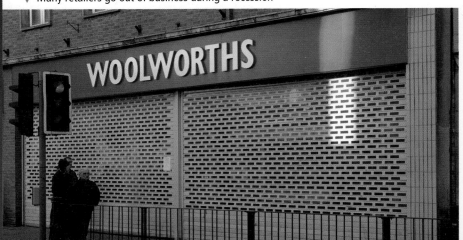

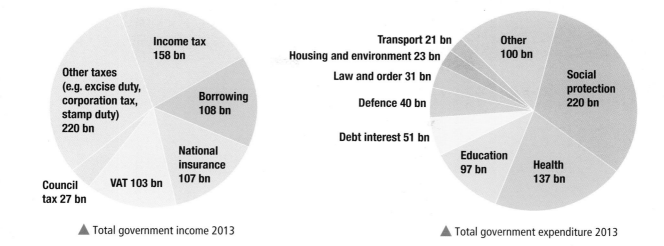

▲ Total government income 2013

▲ Total government expenditure 2013

Government taxation

The government uses the way in which it collects and spends money to control the economy. The way the government collects money is known as taxation. Taxes come in two main forms – direct taxation and indirect taxation.

Direct taxation involves paying a percentage of the money you earn. Examples of direct taxation include income tax and national insurance. Most people pay 20% of what they earn over £10,000 in income tax, plus 12% in national insurance. Earnings over £42,000 are taxed at 40% and over £150,000 at 45%. Direct taxes help poor people because the rich pay more.

Indirect taxation is money paid to the government indirectly. It is a tax on goods or services that you buy. The main form of indirect taxation is VAT – value added tax.

On most goods and services in the UK we pay 20% VAT. Some goods, such as books, food and children's clothes, are not subject to VAT.

Some people think that direct taxation is fairer, because people pay according to how much they earn. Others think that indirect taxation is fairer because people pay according to how much they consume.

Government expenditure

There are many different areas where the government spends money (see above). The biggest area is social security. This includes paying benefits to people who are too ill to work, or who are unemployed.

Government expenditure can boost different parts of the UK economy. For example, in recent years successive governments have increased spending on the NHS.

The person in control of government expenditure and taxation (the Chancellor of the Exchequer) manages the department that controls expenditure and taxation. This is called the Treasury.

Sometimes a government will spend more than it raises in taxation. In order to fund this, the government has to borrow money. This is known as the public sector borrowing requirement.

In groups

Imagine you are members of the government. In order to raise more money to pay off the increased debt resulting from borrowing money during the recession you are going to have to raise taxes. Which taxes will you raise – direct taxes or indirect taxes?

Role play

You are all members of the cabinet in charge of a department such as education, health, defence, housing or transport. In order to balance its budget, the government is going to have to make spending cuts. Hold a discussion in which you argue that the cuts should not be made to your department's spending.

How the global economy works

Aim To examine global economic development and how globalisation has brought both benefits and problems

How the global economy works

The global economy works like the UK national economy. However, it is on a much larger scale. In the same way that certain firms specialise in products and services, so do certain countries. Different countries have different strengths in different areas. For example, the UK is a world leader in biotechnology and pop music. Japan is famous for producing electronic goods, like TVs and computer games. Switzerland is famous for its watches, chocolate and banking services. Brazil is famous for its coffee.

Globalisation

The world economy has been driven by globalisation. Globalisation is the rise in interdependency between countries and companies. This means that both become more dependent or reliant on one another. As companies and countries specialise in different goods and services, they achieve larger economies of scale. This means that on a global scale companies and countries can save millions of pounds by specialising in certain areas. This has been the main driving force of economic growth around the world since the Second World War.

Case study: the fashion industry

Big name celebrities can earn up to £50,000 a day advertising a particular brand, while garment workers in Bangladesh earn hardly enough to live on.

The fashion industry provides an example of how globalisation produces winners and losers.

The winners are the huge companies that have developed brands that are sold in outlets around the world at a price which ensures them a sizeable profit, to be shared among their shareholders.

The losers are the garment makers in countries such as Bangladesh, who are paid only a fraction of the price at which the garments are sold.

On your own

Research the changes in the car industry that have occurred in recent years due to globalisation and how different parts of the manufacturing process now often take place in several different countries rather than all in one country. Then share your findings in a class discussion.

Problems in the global economy

Globalisation has its drawbacks. Interdependency means that a problem in one company or country can have wide and far-reaching effects. For example, there are the dangers of a monopoly. The oil trade is dominated by a few countries, such as Saudi Arabia, which have joined together to form OPEC – the Organisation of Petroleum Exporting Countries. Critics argue that OPEC keeps the price of oil high, to maximise its profits.

When the price of oil is high, the price of petrol goes up in the UK. This makes it more expensive to transport goods in the UK, which means the price of goods has to be raised, making them more difficult to sell.

In addition, countries with more money can dominate those with less. Groups such as Oxfam have criticised countries with more money (such as the UK and USA) for dominating poorer countries (such as Kenya in Africa and Chile in South America).

Finally, companies and countries can lose the ability to produce other goods and services themselves.

THE CREDIT CRUNCH

In 2008, it became apparent that banks around the world had lent too much money to people who could not afford to pay it back. This was especially the case in the poorer parts of America, where people could not pay back their mortgages. As a result, the banks were losing money, and so stopped lending to one another.

The results of this were catastrophic. Businesses could not borrow money, and therefore could not invest to expand. Consumers could not borrow money as easily, so it became much harder for housebuyers to get a mortgage. This became known as the credit crunch in the UK, and resulted in the longest recession in the UK since records began, with businesses failing and unemployment rising.

In pairs

Imagine if the largest industry in your area suddenly had its supply of raw materials cut off because a natural disaster occurred in the country where the raw materials were produced. Draw up lists of what the effects would be. Then compare your lists in a class discussion.

For your file

Discuss as a class what effect the credit crunch had in your area on businesses and consumers. Then each write an explanation of what the credit crunch was and what its effects were in your part of the UK.

How the global economy works

Aim To examine how free trade has created economic growth, bringing prosperity to some countries but not to others

Free trade

Free trade is the idea that there should be as few rules as possible when it comes to international trade. Countries produce the goods and services that they are best at and trade these for things they are less good at producing or cannot produce at all. This free movement of goods and services allows companies to achieve a profit without restriction, as they compete with each other equally around the world. The system is driven by profit and encourages economic growth.

In practice, such perfect competition does not exist, but certain international organisations such as the World Trade Organisation (WTO) are trying to make the rules as equal as possible.

Free trade = unequal trade

With each country specialising in what it is best at producing and selling, free trade should benefit all countries. But in fact, free trade has resulted in very unequal trade. In the last 20 years, the world's 48 poorest countries (with 10% of the world's population) have seen their exports decline to less than half a per cent of the world total, while the US and European countries (with roughly the same number of people) account for 50% of the world's exports.

Subsidies and tariffs

Richer, more powerful countries give subsidies (financial aid) to their own producers. In the US, cotton growers receive subsidies of billions of dollars. This lowers the price of cotton, and producers in Africa and Asia are forced to sell their cotton at a reduced price. Subsidies also mean that farmers produce more than they need, so as to get a higher subsidy. The surplus is then dumped on poorer countries, often at a lower price than it would cost local farmers to produce.

Rich countries also use tariffs (taxes on imports or exports) to protect each other's trading interests by putting higher tariffs on goods manufactured in poorer countries than on goods made in other rich countries.

Source: adapted from www.globalfootprints.org

Free trade and the environment

Free trade can also be harmful to the environment. In the past our fresh food was produced by local farmers. This was because fresh food is perishable and it could not be transported long distances without going off. But today, the transport of food by air, together with new methods of harvesting, storage and refrigeration, means that the food in our shops comes from all over the world. The energy involved and carbon dioxide emitted in transporting food all over the world has an enormous effect on the environment.

In groups

Discuss what free trade is and how in practice free trade benefits rich countries rather than poor countries. Talk about how rich countries use subsidies and tariffs to protect their interests and what effect their use has on poorer countries.

For your file

"The benefits of free trade outweigh the negative effects."

Say why you agree or disagree with this statement.

Economic growth

Because of the size of the global economy, different areas benefit or lose out. Richer countries that have developed their economies are growing richer. These are known as More Economically Developed Countries (MEDCs), and include the USA, Germany, France, the UK and Japan.

There are also Less Economically Developed Countries (LEDCs). These include countries such as the Sudan in Africa, and Afghanistan in Asia. These countries are becoming relatively poorer as the more developed countries continue to grow and prosper.

However, there are some countries, such as China and India, that do not fall into either category. This is because their economies have grown rapidly in recent years and are continuing to grow.

Case study: China

China now has an economy that is growing rapidly, often by 7% a year, a rate unheard of in the UK. China's economy is driven by a booming manufacturing sector, which sends goods to other countries who buy them. These goods are known as China's exports. This is because China is in the middle of an industrial and telecommunications revolution, which is changing its economy – and its society – rapidly.

Case study: India

India is going through a similar process to China, but at a slower pace. While India is behind China in terms of development, both countries are likely to become major economic superpowers by the middle part of the 21st century. This is because of their population. Already, 1 in 4 people in the world lives in China and 1 in 6 in India. In the next few decades, it is predicted that India will overtake China as the world's most populated country. This means that both countries have huge potential markets.

India's rapid growth has not solved all of its problems. Although many people have been lifted out of poverty, large numbers of the population remain poor. Many workers receive low pay and are not allowed to form unions to negotiate for better pay and conditions. Health and safety standards are often poor and the environment suffers from pollution by industries.

For your file

Use the Internet to research what China's economy and society were like 50 years ago and how they have changed in recent years. Write two or three paragraphs on China and how its trade with the rest of the world has increased and how it has developed as an economic power.

In groups

Discuss what MEDCs and LEDCs are. Why do China and India not fit into either category? List the problems that India still faces in spite of its rapid growth.

How the global economy works

Aim To understand multinational corporations, their benefits and drawbacks, and how exploitation of workers can amount to economic slavery

Multinational corporations

A business organisation with its headquarters in one country and operations in many different countries is known as a multinational corporation. Examples of multinational corporations are car manufacturers such as Toyota, oil companies such as Shell, technology companies such as Microsoft, and food and drink companies such as Coca Cola and McDonalds.

Multinationals are huge organisations that operate worldwide. Marks and Spencer sources its goods from over 70 countries.

A multinational corporation often obtains its raw materials in one or more countries, manufactures its product in other countries, and has retail outlets in several countries. This allows the company to buy its raw materials where they are cheapest and to produce its goods where the labour costs are lowest. This in turn maximises its profits.

Many multinational companies buy from local producers in a country, rather than set up factories in that country. The sportswear company Nike is one example. It keeps its costs down by getting local producers to agree to make a specific range of Nike products.

DO MULTINATIONALS HELP OR HARM?

Multinationals can help a country in several ways:
- By bringing money into a country through investment and taxation.
- By creating new jobs which helps reduce poverty.
- By creating a more skilled workforce through training and the introduction of new techniques.
- By investing in improvements to the country's infrastructure (e.g. its roads, railway or port facilities) in addition to its other investments.

But they can also harm...
- By condoning human rights abuse (e.g. sourcing products from factories where child labour is used).
- By damaging the environment through pollution.
- By introducing skilled workers from other countries, rather than training local workers.
- Because the money brought into the country by the multinational corporation may be misused by a corrupt or inefficient government.

Source: www.CAFOD.co.uk

In groups

Discuss what multinational corporations are and how they operate. List the advantages and disadvantages that the operations of a multinational corporation can bring to a country.

In pairs

1 Imagine you work in the PR department of a multinational corporation, MEGA, which plans to invest £100 million in a new factory in a less economically developed country, Poorerland. Draft a press release listing the benefits that MEGA's investment will bring to Poorerland.

2 Imagine you work for a charity that is campaigning to make people aware of the harm that a multinational corporation may do in a country where it operates. Design a poster to draw attention to the drawbacks of multinational corporations.

Problems with multinational corporations

Multinational corporations can create problems. For instance, they can suddenly close a factory in one country and relocate to another for cheaper labour. This means that they are able to drive down wages across the world, which can lead to the exploitation of workers.

Similarly, a government may wish to raise more money by increasing business taxes. However, this may backfire in the case of multinational corporations, because they could simply relocate their operations elsewhere in order to avoid the higher taxes. And as the company leaves, the government ends up with less tax revenue.

The problems in dealing with multinational corporations are difficult for two reasons. Firstly, there will always be a country somewhere that will offer businesses a better deal in terms of rules or taxation. Secondly, multinational corporations have considerable resources, and are therefore very good at lobbying and persuading governments to have rules and taxes that are favourable to them.

Case study: economic slavery

Sometimes workers who produce goods receive virtually no money in wages. For example, in some south-east Asian countries, there are workers doing machining in factories, such as stitching footballs. They work long hours for only a few pence. Meanwhile, the footballs are sold for several pounds in more developed countries. This leads to large profits for the companies involved.

Sometimes children are used who should be at school. This is because with smaller hands they are better at carrying out detailed stitching. These children do not receive a fair share of the profits, but neither do they receive a proper education, so they are exploited twice over.

Role play

You are directors of a multinational corporation who have been told by the government of a country in which you have a large factory employing 1000 people that in future you will have to pay twice as much tax. Some of you argue that you should, therefore, relocate to another country. Others argue that you have a social responsibility to the workforce at the existing factory and that you should stay put, even though profits will be reduced.

For your file

Research other examples of economic slavery on the Internet. Then write an email protesting about the exploitation of workers, in particular child workers.

Aim To understand what fair trade is and how the Ethical Trading Initiative works to improve the working conditions of workers around the world

Fair trade

Fair trade is an alternative trading system designed to protect workers around the world from being exploited by companies, and poorer countries from being exploited by richer ones. The problem arises because of the unequal amount of wealth across the world. For example, a banana company can fix the price it pays small farmers who produce the bananas at a low level. The banana producers have little money or few alternatives, so they are forced to accept the low price. This means they get a small, disproportionate share of the profits when the bananas are eventually sold abroad.

Fair trade is about giving ordinary workers a fair share of the profits, wherever they live or wherever they work in less developed countries. This is done by forming workers into groups of co-operatives. For example, all the banana farmers in an area can group together and then demand a higher price for their bananas from the export company.

Alternatively, they can even contact a distribution company in another country, to sell the bananas directly to them and cut out anyone in the middle. As a result, the co-operative may be able to sell a bunch of bananas for 40p per bunch, rather than 10p previously. This greatly improves their income, and gives them a fair share of the profits.

Protecting the environment

Fair trade can also be used to encourage farmers to farm in a way that is environmentally friendly. For example, the co-operative can state that it will only accept farmers who practise sustainable farming, which means not using chemicals, and using traditional farming methods that do not damage the land. By doing this, the environment is protected for future generations of farmers and consumers.

Case study: Comfort Kumeah

Comfort Kumeah is a mother with five children. and three grandchildren. As well as farming cocoa beans, Comfort also teaches at her local primary school. She lives in a small town in the Ashanti region of Ghana, and she is a member of Kuapa Kokoo cocoa farmers union, a co-operative with 45,000 members. Kuapa sells some of its cocoa to Divine Chocolate Ltd who manufacture Divine and Dubble Fairtrade chocolate bars. The farmers not only receive a fair price, but, unlike other Fairtrade farmers, they also own 45% of the company, which means they enjoy a share of the profits.

"Before, we farmers were cheated. The people who bought from us adjusted the scales and gave us very little money. I joined Kuapa because I saw it was the only organisation which could solve some of our problems – they trade without cheating, with the welfare of farmers at heart. Fairtrade deserves its name because it is fair."

Source: www.divinechocolate.com

In groups

1 Discuss what the fair trade system is and how it works.

2 Design a leaflet to explain what fair trade means in order to persuade people to change their shopping habits and to buy more Fairtrade products.

3 Find out what you can do to become a Fairtrade School on the website: www.fairtrade.org.uk

What is the Ethical Trading Initiative?

The Ethical Trading Initiative (ETI) is an alliance of companies, trade unions and voluntary organisations, working together to improve the lives of workers across the globe who make or grow consumer goods – everything from tea to T-shirts, from flowers to footballs.

What is ethical trading?

Ethical trading means that retailers, brands and their suppliers take responsibility for improving the working conditions of the people who make the products they sell. Most of these workers are employed by supplier companies around the world, many of them in countries where laws designed to protect workers' rights are inadequate or not enforced.

Companies with a commitment to ethical trading adopt a code of labour practice that they expect all their suppliers to work towards, in terms of wages, hours of work, health and safety and the right to join free trades unions.

Practising ethical trading is much harder than it sounds. Modern supply chains are vast and span the globe, and labour issues alone are challenging. For example, what exactly is 'a living wage'? What should a company do if it finds children working in a supplier's worksite? Evicting children from the workplace can, paradoxically, make their lives worse.

The ETI Base Code

The ETI has produced a code of labour practice, known as the ETI Base Code. It consists of 9 basic practices for companies to adopt.

1 Employment is freely chosen. (No one is to be forced to work or lodge a 'deposit' or their identity papers with their employer.)
2 Freedom of association and the right to collective bargaining are respected. (Workers have the right to form or join a trade union.)
3 Working conditions are safe and hygienic.
4 Child labour shall not be used.
5 Living wages are paid.
6 Working hours are not excessive.
7 No discrimination is practised.
8 Regular employment is provided.
9 No harsh or inhumane treatment is allowed. (Physical abuse, sexual harassment, verbal abuse and intimidation are prohibited.)

On your own

Prepare a two-minute talk explaining what the Ethical Training Initiative is, how important you think it is, and why everyone should support it. Then form small groups and take it in turns to give your talk. Decide whose talk is the most informative and most convincing.

For your file

"I had almost 15% of my monthly wage deducted and was given a written warning, because I was 15 minutes late back from lunch." Male worker in a Vietnamese footwear factory

Write an email to send to both the employer and the corporation that uses the factory as a supplier, protesting about the man's treatment.

Source: www.ethicaltrade.org

What you have learned

Aim To review and record what you have learned from studying the units in *Your Life 5*

How to use this section

- Think about what you have learned in each of the five sections of the course.

- Use the questions below on each section to draft a statement about the knowledge and skills you have developed from studying the units in that section.

- In your statements include any important views, expressing the attitudes and values that you have formed as a result of considering and discussing particular topics.

Here's what Corine wrote as part of her statement about what she had learned from the unit on marriage and commitment.

> "It made me realise that just because you're attracted to someone and are in love with them, there are lots of other things to consider before you commit yourself to getting married. I learned a lot about relationships and how to make them work, for example, how important it is to communicate with your partner, especially to say what you really think and feel about difficult issues. It also taught me that you need to think about how you'd both deal with any changes that arise during your marriage, like becoming parents."

Section 1 — **Personal wellbeing – Understanding yourself and handling relationships**

Use these questions to help you draft a statement about what you learned from this section.

What did you learn …
- about developing your own values (pages 6–9)
- about managing your time and studies (pages 10–13)
- about marriage and commitment (pages 14–17)
- about parenthood and parenting (pages 18–21)
- about thinking ahead and planning your future (pages 22–27)?

Section 2 — **Social education – Responsibilities and values**

Use these questions to help you draft a statement about what you learned from this section.

What did you learn …
- about human rights issues (pages 28–33)
- about the global issues of poverty, health and education (pages 34–39)
- about media matters (pages 40–45)
- about challenging offensive behaviour (pages 46–49)?

Section 3 — **Keeping healthy**

Use these questions to help you draft a statement about what you learned from this section.

What did you learn …
- about managing stress and dealing with depression (pages 50–53)
- about safer sex (pages 54–57)
- about drugs and drug taking (pages 58–61)
- about emergency first aid (pages 62–65)?

Section 4 Citizenship – Becoming an active citizen

Use these questions to help you draft a statement about what you learned from this section.

What did you learn ...
- about the UK's role in the world **(pages 66–75)**
- about global issues of wars, weapons and terrorism **(pages 76–81)**
- about global environmental issues **(pages 82–85)**
- about working for change **(pages 86–89)**
- about co-operating on a community project **(pages 90–93)**?

Section 5 Citizenship – Economic and financial capability

Use these questions to help you draft a statement about what you learned from this section.

What did you learn ...
- about managing your money **(pages 94–97)**
- about the UK economy **(pages 98–101)**
- about the global economy **(pages 102–109)**?

Index